THE BUTTERICK
HOME DECORATING HANDBOOK

THE Butterick HOME DECORATING HANDBOOK

A Consumer's Guide
to Selecting, Purchasing, and Caring
for Home Furnishings

Irene Cumming Kleeberg

Published by
BUTTERICK PUBLISHING
A Division of American Can Company
New York, New York 10013

Contents

Introduction

Home is where we spend most of our time, where we feel most ourselves, whether alone or with our families or our friends. Nevertheless, we often find ourselves confused when we think of decorating our homes. Faced by upholstery terms, descriptions of wood finishes, words referring to period decorating, phrases such as *queen size*, paint color choices, fabric selections, and all the other elements that go into decorating a home, we feel lost in a bewildering maze.

This is perfectly understandable. During the twentieth century, and especially within the last thirty years, there have been many technical developments which mean that traditional assumptions about home decorating are no longer valid. Upholstered furniture, for instance, is no longer always made in the conventional way. Wood furniture, too, has changed in construction. Rugs have changed in fiber composition and method of manufacture; paints have changed in formulation. Floor coverings now include synthetic tiles, glass doors may not be glass at all, and window panes have grown to picture windows.

Furthermore, ideas about what our homes should look like have changed. The entire decorating profession has developed over the last fifty years. Magazines devoted exclusively to decorating are proliferating, presenting rooms designed to inspire us all in decorating our homes. Too often, unfortunately, instead of inspiring, these publications may overwhelm us. We sometimes feel we are being told one minute to throw everything out and live with stark modernity and the next to buy it all back — at a greatly inflated price, of course — and turn our homes into replicas of cluttered Victoriana.

This isn't really happening, of course. The decorating magazines are showing us the variety of possibilities we have in choosing how we dress our homes. The problem is that because so many new developments have come along, we feel we lack the knowledge necessary to buy for our homes wisely.

This book is designed primarily as a consumer guide to the confusing world of home decorating. It is not designed to suggest to you specific room settings or floor plans that you can copy, but to give you the information you'll need to find your own way to the home you want.

HOW TO USE THIS BOOK

The book is divided into sections to help you spend your money and time wisely and well.

At the beginning we give you, in brief form, information that you need to make wise general choices. We discuss decorators and their role, how to work with or without a decorator, what period furniture is, what current decorating trends there are for you to follow or ignore.

We include a section on analyzing the needs of your family so that you can make a home that not only looks right but works right. You'll find that in this way your home will acquire individuality and warmth.

We suggest you start by taking a look at the things you already own. Many of these things — no matter how humble — can be used in a new decorating scheme. We also help you to figure out a buying plan so you won't have to buy everything at once.

Color, texture, and pattern, more than any other elements, give a room its feeling of comfort or awkwardness. We discuss color, including various theories of color, using texture, and bringing a room to life through combining both color and texture with pattern.

The chapters which follow these early ones give more specific advice on purchasing items for your home. Each chapter includes a general discussion of the various items and charts to show you, in capsule form, what is available. We have tried to combine both theory and practice in these chapters, telling you what the ideal is generally agreed to be while at the same time telling you what you may have to settle for when you go to buy.

There are many new developments in furniture, ranging from the increasing use of fabric over plastic foam to the increasing variety of unpainted furniture, which have been ignored by most experts. We cover these and other such subjects in this book.

Our chapter on room backgrounds looks at wall coverings, floor coverings, and ceiling treatments. We try to bring you the specific information you will find most helpful in deciding what you want to use where, and how to use it. Window treatments are covered in a separate chapter.

Lighting for the home is another rapidly changing area today. We are becoming more and more aware of how light affects not only our ability to see objects but also our mood. This is thoroughly covered in its own chapter. And we have a special section on the rooms — children's rooms, bathrooms, kitchens, and family rooms — which need special attention.

Accessories, fireplaces, and plants, a decorator once said, are the exclamation points of a room. More than almost anything else, they are personal choices, but we discuss various general possibilities for buying and using them. And we have a chapter on a contemporary concern — energy conservation. We mention energy conservation where appropriate throughout the book, but we group the information together in this chapter and give you additional information on how your decorating can help you save energy in your home.

There's no point in buying home furnishings items and not knowing how to care for them. We have included pointers on the care (and, in the case of wood, the feeding) of the items discussed. We have also included information on spot and stain removal.

Finally, we have a chapter on getting what you want.

This gives you a brief look at the way home furnishings are likely to be divided up in large stores, discusses delivery, and gives you advice about solving problems which may arise.

The dictionary section of the book comes next. This is designed for easy reference. If, for instance, you want to find out what a Barcelona chair is, you would look under *Barcelona* and be directed to the word *chair*, where *Barcelona chair* is defined. If you wanted some ideas of general chair possibilities, however, you would start with the word *chair*.

Many terms are used in the industry in ways which are not, strictly speaking, correct. We give you the correct definition first and then the present-day use of the term.

An index completes the book.

In preparing this book for your use, we have been very much aware that home decorating is a constantly changing and developing field. Our goal in this book is to give you the information you'll need to be able to make wise purchases that will please you in your home. We hope you'll find the *Butterick Home Decorating Handbook* useful as you make your way through the often confusing world of home decorating.

1

Don't Be Afraid of Home Decorating

Even in this age of "be natural" and "do-it-yourself," many people are afraid of decorating. If you are, don't worry about it — you're not alone. There are perfectly good reasons for being afraid of decorating. Many items you buy for your home are expensive, at least compared to most of the items you buy every day.

Furthermore, because of the expense and because of tradition, these things are expected to last and last. Although people today often don't want things to last quite as long as they did fifty years ago, we all want to get maximum value for our money. Even though we may say, "We'll buy this now and when we can afford it we'll get something better," it's surprising how long we can find ourselves keeping things. The chair that was bought for four years at college is still around after a twenty-fifth college reunion. The rug that was bought for a first small apartment ends up flooring the children's room. This is why it's best to get something that is both right and attractive even if you do intend to replace it later. The problem is in making sure that the thing is right for you.

Most of us simply don't know very much about the elements that go into decorating our homes, and that's why we're afraid. This book is designed to give you knowledge so that you'll be less afraid of the actual decorating.

WHY DECORATE?

Keep in mind what the purpose of decorating your home is. This is a somewhat tricky question. In theory, it should be to make your home comfortable for you and your family, not to impress the neighbors. In practice, you may want to impress the neighbors to a certain extent, but try to avoid sacrificing too much in the way of comfort and convenience for you and your family.

The simplest way to decorate is to take over someone else's ideas whole. This can mean completely duplicating your mother's house, a magazine picture, or a model room in a store. The more complex way to decorate is to create a home that fits the way you and your family live, a home which is uniquely yours. Most people use others' ideas as a starting point and go on to adapt those ideas so they are right for their own particular situation. If you use that method and keep your decorating options open over a period of years, you'll eventually find that you have created the home that works best for you and your family.

EVOLUTION

You can't build a home decorating plan that will suit you in one step. It has to evolve over a period of time. Your interests and those of your family will change, even if your family consists only of you and your plants.

Your decorating plans should be flexible enough so that you can make changes later with a minimum of upheaval. Furthermore, the type of home you have should also be determined by the amount of space you have. If you have a large house or apartment you can keep one room as an impress-your-neighbors room more easily than if you live in a two-room apartment. You can also have more rooms for specific purposes in a larger house than in a smaller one.

HOW TO START

If you want help in decorating your home (and just about everyone does) there is a lot of help around. Some of it is good, some bad, but you should have enough courage of your convictions to decide which is which before you make a commitment.

MAGAZINES

Magazines are some of the richest sources of decorating ideas. Don't limit your looking only to magazines in the decorating field. You can also get ideas from backgrounds shown in other pictures — on a food page, for instance.

Decorating magazines range from the very elegant to the very practical. Often the price is a guide to the type of information you'll find inside. The more expensive the magazine, the more likely it is to have expensive ideas. Look at all kinds of magazines. You can pick up color schemes or unusual ideas from magazines at both ends of the price scale.

After a time, you'll discover that there are certain absolutes in magazines. Fine French furniture, for instance, is very popular in the more expensive magazines when traditional interiors are shown. When modern interiors appear, sooner or later you'll see the Barcelona chair. Learning to recognize some of these common elements can help you analyze what it is that appeals to you in the various rooms shown. Don't try to remember the things you have seen in these magazines. Instead, clip from the magazines those pictures, colors, patterns, or ideas that seem right to you. This will help you focus your own feelings and learn your own taste.

BOOKS

Books are another source of information and inspiration. Many decorating books are both big and expensive, and expensive ideas are shown in them. However, there are some less expensive, more practical volumes available, usually as large sized paperbacks. Check books carefully before buying. If you find one that seems to answer some of your questions, buy it.

WHAT YOU SEE

Analyze — don't just notice — what you like about various rooms. Look at room settings in department and furniture stores, yes, but also look at your friends' homes, museum rooms, offices, restaurants. When you see a room you like, analyze its appeal by asking yourself, "Is it the color I like? What about the comfort of the seating? The window coverings? The lighting? The contrast of textures?"

In time, you will come to know what you really like. Most of us start out thinking that what we like best is whatever the currently popular decorating trend is, only to find later that our tastes are quite different. If you do enough attentive looking you'll discover what really appeals to you as well as what you consider only "a nice place to visit."

USING DECORATORS

Decorators are another source of help in decorating your home. Decorators are professionals who are experts in planning the decorating of a home. They become experts through formal classroom training, by working as an apprentice to another decorator, or by decorating many rooms. Because decorators are professionals, they can often see in a minute solutions to problems which you might solve only by trial and error.

A decorator, however, needs as much information about you and your family as possible to do a really good job. You should probably wait until you have some preliminary ideas of what you want and what you need before getting in touch with a decorator. Many people successfully decorate their homes with no professional decorating help.

People in the decorating field have begun to frown upon the term *interior decorator* because many people set themselves up as interior decorators although they lack what others in the field consider proper credentials.

Many interior decorators prefer to call themselves interior designers, stressing that they do more than decorate — they also design space so it can be used most effectively.

There were two recognized societies for decorators; they

were the American Institute of Interior Designers (AID) and the National Society of Interior Designers (NSID). The groups have now merged into the American Society of Interior Designers, but many decorators used the old abbreviations. Members of these groups have certain professional qualifications (usually in terms of education and experience) which set a minimum standard. However, many of the best decorators and designers, including some of the most famous, do not have this training or do not belong to ASID.

STORE DECORATORS

Some decorating services are free, or can be free. For instance, many department and furniture stores have decorating departments. In most cases you do not pay decorators in these departments. They are usually considered part of the stores' services and are paid as salespeople are paid, out of the markup (typically double the wholesale price) the store puts on merchandise. You should find out during your first interview exactly how a store decorator — or any decorator — will be paid.

Some stores which supply free decorating services charge for certain things that a decorator may do for you. For instance, there may be a charge if the decorator paints a picture of the way the room will look when finished (this is called a rendering).

Then, too, the store won't let you take endless hours of a decorator's time only to turn around and buy the items cheap from your brother-in-law.

Decorators — and stores — have to make a living, so occasionally they'll try to protect themselves by having you make a deposit which will be deducted from your order. If you order nothing, this deposit pays for the decorator's services and is usually forfeited. If you do use the services of a store decorator you should be prepared to buy at least $2,000 worth of merchandise from that store. Be sure you know the rules before you start.

Watch out for stores which call all their salespeople decorators. You want to be sure that the decorator you are using knows what's what. Membership in ASID is one indication, but more important is the impression the decorator makes on you.

INDEPENDENT DECORATORS

The second type of decorator is the one who sets up his own independent business. Here, the decorator usually buys wholesale and sells to you at retail.

If he supervises such jobs as the painting of your walls, or if he does any type of labor or provides labor for you, he is likely to charge you more than you would pay if you hired directly. This is because it requires both time and work to supervise someone.

The same thing is true if a decorator spends a lot of time looking for something special such as an antique comb-and-brush set for your dressing table. You might have been able to find it in the same antique shop the decorator found it in — and if you had, you might have bought it for less than you will pay him. But the decorator did the running around looking for it and — often more important — knew where to run. This is something you could learn only after putting in years of this kind of shopping as, of course, the decorator has done. You may be charged by the hour for this type of searching. The figure is usually about $50 an hour, but it varies from decorator to decorator and city to city. Again, ask before you agree to anything.

There are also decorators who will provide you with a rendering of what your room will look like when finished, to give you color direction and perhaps furniture ideas, but will not do the actual work of getting the painters to follow his color scheme (instead of their own), or scream at the furniture manufacturer to get your furniture delivered on schedule. Except in relatively rare cases when renderings are offered free in the hope that customers will later purchase items through the decorator, a fee is charged, usually based on the time spent on the project.

DISCOUNT DECORATORS

There are other decorators frowned on by the leaders in the industry. These decorators are people who have merely set themselves up as decorators for the purpose of buying furniture wholesale and then selling it to you at a discount. They take a smaller percentage than the usual 50 percent markup and sell the item to you at a good deal less than the usual retail price.

Again, as in the case of the ordinary store salesperson who is called a decorator, you get no other service from such a decorator. You get no advice or, if you do, it should be regarded suspiciously, as the advice may be to use a company which gives this decorator a bigger discount.

Despite the feelings that other decorators have toward discount decorators, there are some occasions when it is sensible to use them. If, for example, you fall in love with an extremely expensive piece of furniture and want that and no other, there's no reason why you shouldn't try to get it for less money. The danger is in assuming that the advice of discounters — rather than just their purchasing ability — is worth anything to you.

TALK FIRST

Don't jump to use any kind of decorator just because you think it would necessarily be simpler — or more fashionable — to use one. Instead, talk to the decorator first and discover exactly what fees are involved and how they will be determined. Make sure that you are both clear on how much money you want to spend.

If fees are based on time spent, double any estimate. Do this because you will probably overestimate the ease of decorating your home, and so will the decorator. We often think things will take less time than they usually do.

Have the first interview, by telephone or in person, to set down and make clear the ground rules. Explain before the interview that all you want to do is find out the fees. Remember that the decorator's time is money, so don't waste it. And, of course, don't try to get free advice during this interview. Don't get into your specific decorating problems yet.

DO YOU NEED A DECORATOR?

There's no question that a good decorator can save you time and energy; there is some question as to whether or not a

HOW TO FIND AND USE DECORATING HELP

Type	Where Found	Use
Magazines	Newsstands; libraries	Source of decorating trends, color ideas, floor plans, room uses
Books	Bookstores; libraries	Similar to above, but often more detailed
Model rooms	Department stores; furniture stores; housing developments	Source of decorating ideas, information on currently available furniture
Museum rooms	Major museums with furniture collections; reconstructed or preserved communities and houses	Information on historical decorating
Decorators	Department and furniture stores	Advice on planning and purchasing decorating items
	Independent	Same
	Discount	Discount purchasing of decorating items

HOW TO FIND AND USE DECORATING HELP

Advantages	Disadvantages	Cost
Good source of ideas and current information	Ideas sometimes overly expensive, too dramatic; may only show advertisers' items	$1.00 and up
Trends shown have usually lasted for some time	Ideas often overly expensive; may show one-of-a-kind furniture or room detailing	About $10.00 and up for hardcover books; about $4.00 and up for paperback books
Merchandise shown can be purchased	All merchandise from store's stock only; not always best choice for you	Free
Items shown are usually authentic	May be too rigid or too museumlike if transferred whole to a home	Admission ranges from free to about $2.50
Advice is from trained person; saves time	Merchandise choice mainly limited to store stock	Most of the time free, but you will be expected to buy at least $2,000 worth of merchandise
Same	Decorator earns commission on each item sold, so may pressure clients	Same as above
Saves money	No advice or relatively poor advice	Free (decorator makes money on commission)

decorator will save you money. This is only logical — decorators want to make money and many won't work on very limited budgets. Furthermore, they don't have much incentive to find cheap sources of furniture and fabric since, in most cases, the more you spend the more they will earn — a percentage of the selling price is paid to the decorator as a commission. There is nothing wrong with this so long as you understand it.

Even though a professional decorator will save you time and will probably come up with many excellent ideas for solving specific problems, you will have to work hard with the decorator both before the work starts and while your home is being decorated. Otherwise, you won't get what you want.

In the next chapter you will find a listing of things to consider in decorating whether you are using a decorator or not. If you do the right kind of pre-thinking and pre-planning, you can be equally successful in doing your own decorating or using a decorator. It becomes, then, a question that involves time as well as money. If you find you enjoy the searching and can afford to spend the time in decorating that a professional could save you, you may be happier doing your own decorating. If you have an extremely limited budget, you may also want to do your own decorating. If, on the other hand, you have both unlimited time and a fairly large budget, the decision becomes a matter of priorities and you may well decide to use a decorator because of the experience such a professional can bring to your own home.

2

Knowing Yourself and Your Family

Knowing yourself and your family is the most important element in decorating your home. Whether or not you use a decorator, this knowledge is essential for success.

Any decorator will want to be sure that anything planned is right for you, and the way to be sure it is right is to ask you a lot of questions about you, your family, and your life. If you are being your own decorator, you will still have to face and answer these questions. Even if you are only buying a single table you will be happier with that table if you have taken these steps.

START WITH THE BASICS

Start with the absolute basics of your life. Ask yourself what you want to do in your home. At its simplest you'll probably come up with four answers — sleep, eat, wash, and relax. These answers suggest other questions.

At the end of this chapter you'll find a chart. One is designed for you to use in considering the decorating needs of the members of your family. We show this chart both made out for a mythical family and blank for you to fill in with your own answers.

SLEEPING

Sleeping means beds or, at least, a bedroll on the floor.

A bed can be a formal bed, such as a four-poster, a mattress on the floor with a colorful throw over it, a sofa bed in what is otherwise the living room, double-decker bunk beds, or a deck over a dining table.

For a baby, a place to sleep can be a bassinet, a bureau drawer (taken out of the bureau, of course), a crib, a play pen, a carriage. After the baby is about three months old, the possibilities are pretty much limited to either a crib or a playpen. Most parents prefer a crib.

Sleeping requires certain things — ideally, quiet, darkness, comfort.

Does it also require a room reserved only for sleeping? If you have a large house, yes. But if you have a two-room apartment and two children, you may end up on a sofa bed in the living room.

Do you like to read in bed? Do you like to eat in bed? Then you'll need a reading light of some kind, and perhaps a cooky jar.

You'll probably need some storage space near your sleeping place. You may be able to make a chest of drawers work as a bedside table.

It's generally agreed that it's best for everyone to have his own bedroom — everyone, that is, except people who are married to each other, roommates in college or at work, children in a small house or apartment. Work out what seems best for you and your family, keeping in mind, however, that most children prefer to have a room of their own, however small and cut up it may be, rather than share a room with anyone else.

WASHING

Washing is simple — or should be. It means a bathroom, and the bathroom is already part of your home. With it, the main questions are true decorating questions: whether to add plants or a shelf of magazines, whether to have a red shower curtain, a glass enclosure, or to coordinate everything to the color of your favorite bath salts.

Washing also includes washing dishes. Will that be done by hand? In a dishwasher? In the kitchen?

And washing includes washing clothes. Where will that be done? In the basement? At a laundromat? By hand? By machine? How will they dry? Where?

EATING

Eating is another activity. Eating requires a kitchen where the food can be cooked, and the kitchen, like the bathroom, is usually something you find already there when you move into a house or apartment.

Where will you eat the meals that come from the kitchen? Do you think it's fun and informal to eat all your meals in the kitchen, or do you think the kitchen is only right for eating breakfast? Is the kitchen big enough to eat in if you want to?

Do you have a dining room? Do you want to keep it as a dining room or turn it to some other use? Do you want a formal dining room table? Do you want to eat at one end of the living room, or would that seem too much like camping out to you?

RELAXING

When we get to the next section, relaxing, we bring up a great many more questions. One person's relaxation is another's plain hard work. If your idea of relaxation is reading, your hobby is fairly easy to cater for — except that you'll probably want a degree of quiet, a degree of comfort, a place to keep books, and good lighting.

Do you like to sew? Then you'll need a place for the sewing machine, a place for the ironing board, a full-length mirror. Do you like carpentry work? Then you'll need a place for tools, a workbench, and so forth.

How about listening to music? Can you do that without disturbing the rest of the family? In a large house, you may be able to set aside a room as a music or noise room. In a small apartment, your answer may be to be sure no noise-making item (radio, television, record player) comes without a place to plug in a pair of earphones.

Keep the children — if any — in mind, too. It's terrific if they can have one place to keep as messy as they want (their own rooms, perhaps) until there's a grand (usually adult-inspired) cleanup.

WORKING

For many people, being at home includes working, just as it does for school children with homework. You may bring work home from the office, run volunteer activities, write novels, run a travel service. If you have children, it's probably best to have your working area away from their play area. Of course, this isn't always possible. If you're the only person around to look after them you can't very well isolate yourself from them behind an office door, and it becomes a matter of trying for quiet when you're working.

One successful solution we know involved perching a writing mother on a high stool. Her children knew that when she was up there emergencies would be attended to but she was by and large not available.

BE FLEXIBLE

One of the most important elements in working out your thoughts before decorating is to keep your solutions flexible. Keep your own attitude flexible too, so that as needs change the uses of various rooms can change.

It may be that in the early years of your children's lives you'll turn the dining room into a playroom for them. When they go to school, the toys-on-the-floor period should be almost over, and the dining room could be turned over to homework.

Later still, as the children grow older and are out of the house more, that same dining room can be turned into a family room — for rug making, sewing, woodworking, pottery, painting.

And, later still, if you've been hankering all those years after a dining room, there's no reason at all why it can't be reincarnated once again as what it was intended to be — a formal dining room.

The point of all this preliminary questioning and thinking about your family needs is to keep you from finding yourself with a gorgeous decorator showcase that doesn't take into account either the actual space of your home or the needs of your family.

OTHER PEOPLE

The family comes first in your thinking, but the other people who come to your home are part of your life, too. However homey home may be, we don't want it to be a place where there's never room to have company.

How often do you entertain? What type of entertaining is it? If you like to have two other couples in for dinner you'll need less area for entertaining than if you like to have 150 people in for cocktails twice a year.

Keep in mind that furniture arrangements are designed to work for you, not against you. If you like a way of arranging the furniture but feel it would make entertaining impossible, figure out if it can easily be rearranged for entertaining, by using casters, for example.

Although ideally the purpose of your home is to be right for you and your family, you may get involved in a certain amount of entertaining that requires a special setting.

This can be solved by setting aside one room — formal or informal — for such entertaining. This is a hangover from the old days of the parlor, which was used only for formal visiting.

If you have the space and like the idea of entertaining in a completely different setting from where you live, go ahead and plan such a special room. If you like the idea but can't afford a special room, look into the possibility of renting space outside your home for such occasions.

The following charts are designed to help you ask yourself the questions you will need to answer to arrive at a satisfactory decorating plan.

NEEDS OF FAMILY MEMBERS
(Filled Out for Mythical Family)

	Sleeping	Eating	Washing	Working	Relaxing, Hobbies
Self	Sofa bed in living room	Table in living room	Large bathroom; kitchen; laundromat	Desk; space for typewriter; files	Reading: comfortable chair; good lighting; sewing: machine — storage space; full-length mirror
Spouse	Sofa bed in living room	Table in living room	Large bathroom	Desk; files	Reading in bed: good light; listening to music in bed: earphones; record collecting: earphones, space for equipment; record storage
Child I	Bed in own bedroom	Table in living room	Small bathroom	Desk; book shelves	Reading in bed: good light; television: earphones; darts: space for dart board; plants: bright window
Other adult	Bed in own bedroom	Table in living room; table in own room	Small bathroom	Desk	Television: earphones; writing letters (see working); entertaining (see eating)

NEEDS OF FAMILY MEMBERS
(Fill Out for Yourself)

	Sleeping	Eating	Washing	Working	Relaxing, Hobbies
Self					
Spouse					
Child I					
Child II					
Child III					
Child IV					
Roommate I					
Roommate II					
Other Adult I					
Other Adult II					
Pets					

3

Start with What You Have

Most of us start decorating our homes with at least a little more than empty spaces and a fistful of money. We have some possessions — a chair, a rug, a family picture, a bookcase. We usually want to fit these things into a decorating scheme rather than throwing them out, but we wonder if they'll work. This is one side of the "start with what you have" coin. The other side is space. It's important to consider what is available in the way of actual space. And, finally, as a background to these considerations, we have to take into account what we have in the way of money.

YOUR NEEDS

Start by looking at what you found from the study you did of your life and your family. This will give you ideas both of your likes and your needs for living.

In considering your space needs, remember that any space can be used for one thing at one time and another at another. There's no reason why the living room, for instance, can't be used for entertaining, hobbies, eating, and even sleeping. The dining room can be used for working (sewing, studying, writing) as well as eating.

Next, make a list of everything you have that can be used to furnish or decorate the room you are working with. There is a chart at the end of this chapter with space for you to list each item and what you want to do with it. You can copy the format of that chart if you find you need more space than it gives. Until you are sure of the answers, don't fill in all the spaces, or else make the answers tentative by filling in the chart in pencil.

Your next step is to figure out your needs. Here are some suggestions.

THE BARE MINIMUM

Suppose you are starting from scratch to furnish a room, an apartment, or a house. Here is our bare minimum, exclusive of kitchen items. Your own list might be different — this is just to start you thinking.

• *Bed*. You can use it also as a sofa. It can be a single studio bed or a sofa bed which can sleep two.

• *Chair*. It should be both sturdy enough to sit in while writing and comfortable enough for a guest. A Windsor chair works well. Add a cushion if you want.

• *Trunk or very large suitcase*. The footlocker you took to camp as a child or a straw or wicker trunk is perfect. It works as a coffee table or an end table, for extra seating when you need it, and it can also hold some of your clothes.

• *Lamp*. A floor lamp is best so you can move it around the room.

• *Rug*. A rug isn't one of the first things you need, but you should add one when you have more money. It furnishes a room faster than anything else, makes the room seem warmer, and encourages your guests to sit on the floor.

• *Table*. A table, like a rug, isn't one of the first things you need, but should follow soon after the bare essentials. This table should work both as a dining table and as a desk.

• *Chest of drawers*. A chest of drawers, added after the rug and table, will mean you'll have more storage space and can take some of the things out of that trunk.

The next group of items you should buy is up to you.

Think about end tables, bookcases, table lamps, pictures, and mirrors.

SAVING MONEY

If you're very short of cash, look for your first furniture in secondhand shops and thrift shops such as those run by the Salvation Army. In cities check the sidewalks the night before scheduled bulk refuse collections.

Scrounge things from friends and relatives, and never say no. You can always paint or re-cover furniture if you don't like the way it is.

The list of basic furniture above will continue to work as you add more furniture to your total mix or as you add family members. Your children, for instance, will also need beds, chairs, desks or tables, rugs, and chests of drawers in their rooms. You may find that many items from your first home can later be used to furnish your children's rooms.

The difference between living in a small apartment, room, or house and a large place is primarily in quantity — quantity of space, quantity of furniture possible. The biggest practical difference is probably that different activities have their own specific spaces or rooms in a larger home.

Following is a discussion of specific rooms with specific functions.

LIVING ROOM POSSIBILITIES

Start with the living room — it is the most important room in most homes. If, for instance, you live in a one-room apartment, your aim in decorating will be to give that apartment the appearance of being one large living room.

In the living room your first goal will probably be to create a setting where at least three people can sit comfortably and talk. This can be a sofa with a chair or two, a built-in window or wall seat, three chairs, or, at its simplest, three big cushions on the floor. If you live in a one-room apartment or a dormitory room and use the bed as a sofa, two people can sit on the edge of the bed and you'll need only one chair.

SEATING ARRANGEMENTS

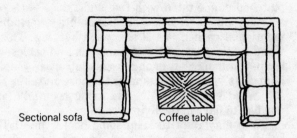

Sectional sofa   Coffee table

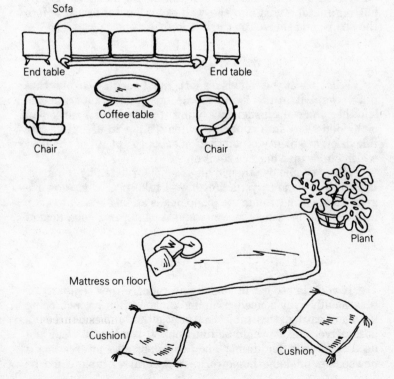

Sofa

End table   End table

Coffee table

Chair   Chair

Plant

Mattress on floor

Cushion   Cushion

Even if you plan to use another room for most of your entertaining, as part of this grouping you'll need a place for people to put things — books, ashtrays, glasses, snacks. A matched coffee table with two end tables is the conventional solution, but there are other possibilities, including the trunk mentioned earlier. You'll also need lighting. This can be provided by floor lamps, table lamps on end tables, or a hanging lamp, if it hangs low enough to be flattering. (Light that is too high casts ugly shadows under the nose and chin.)

What else goes on in the living room? What else would you like to have in the living room?

You may want to keep some books there. That means a bookcase or bookcases. A bookcase can be as elaborate as the top half of an antique secretary or as simple as brick-supported boards. A bookcase can be an expensive built-in early American bookcase or one you install inexpensively by putting metal strips into the wall studs, metal brackets into the strips, and shelves on the brackets.

TELEVISION AND MUSIC

What about the television set? You'll need a place for that if you want it in the living room, and you'll want to decide whether you want it silently looking at you when it's turned off or hidden away in a cupboard when it's not in use. Give any television set plenty of ventilation room to get rid of the heat which builds up when the set is on.

Many people use their living rooms for listening to music. If there's a piano in your life, it will take precedence over a great many other things. A piano needs an inside wall to keep it warm and preserve its tone, and it requires a good deal of space.

EATING AND WORKING

If you plan to eat in your living room, either regularly or occasionally, you'll need a dining table. When it's not being used for eating, this table can play either a functional or a decorative role. It would be functional if you kept it clear and used it strictly for dining and, perhaps, also for reading a newspaper or doing homework. A decorative table could be

DESKS

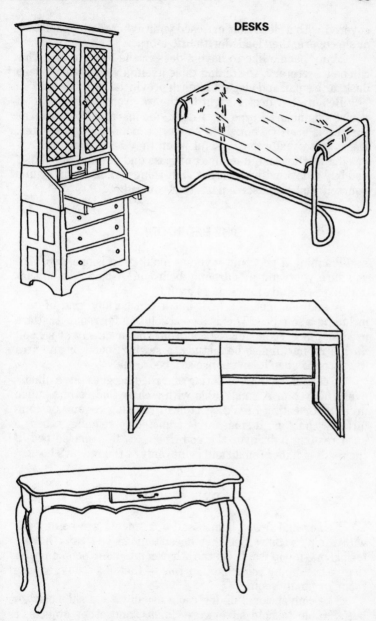

covered with a cloth that matched your living room upholstery or slipcovers, then loaded with bric-a-brac.

Many people like to have a desk in the living room. This can be a secretary, the dining table itself, a very plain modern desk, or a small and elegant French provincial lady's desk.

Be sure any desk is right for the way you plan to use it. If you're planning to type on a desk, for instance, be sure the surface is sturdy enough to support a pounding typewriter. Desks are usually most useful when they have drawers. Appealing as the clean-lined look of glass and chrome may be, if you buy a desk with no place to put things you'll probably find yourself wishing at some point that you hadn't.

THE BEDROOM

Planning a bedroom involves making decisions, too. Are you sure you want a bedroomy bedroom? Would a room that doubled as a study prove more useful?

A bedroom needs a bed, but it can be any kind of bed, including a sofa bed. This is a good solution for rooms that are used as guest rooms or for children who are away at school. Such a room can also be a study, a sewing room, or an extra living room when it isn't in use as a bedroom.

A certain amount of eating and reading goes on in almost every bedroom. A small table with a chair that can be pulled up to it for eating breakfast is nice. Reading requires a comfortable chair or, if someone is addicted to reading in bed, a good reading light over the bed. It's best, in a shared bed, if the reading light is small and points only at the reader's book.

THE DINING ROOM

Fewer and fewer homes and apartments are being built with dining rooms, but that doesn't mean you can't have a formal one if you want. On the other hand, many people prefer to give the dining room another role — that of a study, sewing room, or family room.

The conventional dining room usually has a sideboard or buffet table to hold silverware, linens, and other objects, a large dining table in the center of the room which expands to seat at least twelve people, and chairs around the dining table. There are usually two armchairs, sometimes called host and hostess chairs, with the other chairs, armless, called side chairs.

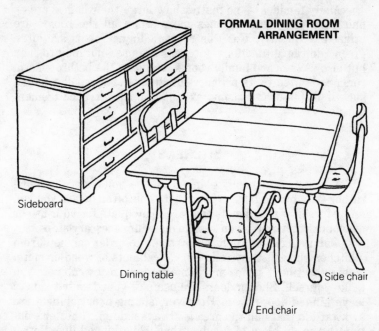

FORMAL DINING ROOM ARRANGEMENT

Sideboard

Dining table

End chair

Side chair

If you plan to buy a conventional dining table, you should be aware that most experts consider a square or rectangular table more practical (it can be pushed against the wall, for instance). On the other hand, these same experts think that round or oval tables are more attractive in appearance and are better for encouraging general table conversation. If you plan to use your table only in the middle of the room, pick a round or oval table if you like the look; otherwise, choose a square or rectangular one.

You may want to add more furniture to your dining room. For instance, a low chest for silver and tablecloths is useful. A corner cupboard is almost required in an early American dining room.

Even if you want to keep your dining room primarily for dining, you should consider using it for some other purposes. Think about putting the television set in the dining room, with a comfortable chair to sit in. Or consider placing the piano or your desk in the dining room.

Many families — no matter how large their homes are — find they enjoy their homes more when all the rooms are utilized frequently. For this reason, dining rooms are often given additional functions, kitchens are used not only to cook but also as informal family rooms, and only the bathroom still remains limited to its primary function. In the smaller home, such multiple use of rooms expands apparent space tremendously.

KITCHENS

Kitchens are usually planned by the builder of the home rather than by the family living in it. This often means you will find yourself with cabinets that are inadequate for your use or a layout that requires you to take many unnecessary steps.

Cabinets can be replaced by made-to-order cabinets from a kitchen specialist, by ready-made cabinets of wood or metal from department stores and home centers, or by cabinets you make yourself. Sliding doors are useful if your family tends to leave hinged doors open. However, sliding-door cabinets are awkward in that half the area is always hidden. A better solution to the problem of families that leave hinged doors open might be to be sure all doors have strong magnetic catches.

Inefficient arrangements of kitchens are fairly common. You may find it worthwhile to move the refrigerator so it is nearer the working area or to supplement the work areas you now have with a permanent or rolling work table.

Many families like to eat at least some of their meals in the kitchen. There are many answers to the question of what to use for these meals. Tables and chairs designed for outdoor use, dinette tables, or conventional dining tables and chairs are all possibilities depending on your budget, the space you have, and your taste. Consider, too, if space is limited, building a counter and using stools with it for eating. The same counter can provide additional work space.

Large, old-fashioned kitchens are becoming popular once again. For such a kitchen, you would probably want to have a large dining table which can also be used for meal planning and homework, perhaps a rocking chair for relaxation. If you have the space, many types of storage items can be added to a kitchen, ranging from a corner cabinet to a deacon's bench used for seating as well as storage.

BATHROOMS

Short of major remodeling, relatively little can be done to change a bathroom in terms of the actual fixtures. A great deal, however, can be done with decorating, through rugs, shower curtains, window curtains, and wall coverings.

Certain furniture items can be added to the bathroom to make it more functional and give it more uses. Metal shelves are available which fit against the wall, hold towels, bath salts, extra soap, and so forth. You can buy towel rings (elegant, although they tend to bunch the towels, making them take longer to dry) which can be attached with screws or glue to the wall. You should certainly plan to close in the bathroom sink to provide you with extra space if it is not already enclosed.

Look at your bathroom for other space-use possibilities. You may find that a cabinet could be fitted over the door to hold all your towels and wash cloths, freeing another area of your storage space for other items. If you have very high ceilings, you might want to build shelving over the bathtub. This only works, of course, in a bathroom where the shower head is well below the area where the bottom of the shelving would be.

TRAFFIC PATTERNS

Traffic flow is almost as important in a home as in a city. Professional decorators spend a good deal of time, consciously or unconsciously, working out traffic patterns.

Traffic patterns is the term used to describe the way in which people will move around your home — from the living room to the kitchen, for instance, or from the bathroom to the bedrooms. The ideal is to make the traffic patterns logical ones so that people don't have to slow down suddenly in their dash around the house to avoid banging into the furniture.

If possible, the traffic patterns should also be such that there is no need to pass through rooms unnecessarily. If you have a choice of where to place your dining room, for instance, you should choose the room nearest the kitchen so you will not have to pass through the living room to reach the dining room, nor carry food and dishes a distance.

Ideally, any traffic pattern should be in a straight line. A person entering the living room from the kitchen, for instance, should be able to walk in a direct line to the front entrance to the living room. In practice, you may find that the only possible place for the sofa means that the coffee table will jut slightly in the middle of a logical traffic pattern. Try to keep such interruptions in the flow of traffic at a minimum.

In the charts which follow, we have tried to boil down the information here. The first chart is designed for you to list the items you already have; the second chart is designed for you to list the items you feel you need.

Don't arbitrarily decide to throw out things which are perfectly good.

Perhaps that chest of drawers you hate would benefit from being painted emerald green. Perhaps those curtains could be dyed. Maybe the rug that's too small for the living room would look fine in the kids' room. Try various ways of updating and changing items (if only in your head) before deciding they are unusable.

POSSIBLE FAMILY FURNITURE NEEDS
(Compare with fill-in chart, "Needed and Wanted Items," p. 40)

Sleeping	Eating	Relaxing/Hobbies	Working
Mattress	Round table	Chairs	Desk
Full-size bed	Oval table	Sofas	Table
Queen-size bed	Square table	Love seats	Typewriter storage
King-size bed	Rectangular	Recliners	File storage
Twin bed	table	Coffee tables	Stationery storage
Cot	Kitchen table	End tables	
Bunk bed	Counter	Piano	
Sofa bed	Folding trays	Record cabinets	
Crib		Bar	
Bassinet		Plant trays	
		Sport and game	
		supply storage	

Needs

FILL-IN CHART: NEEDED AND WANTED ITEMS
(Compare with "Possible Family Furniture Needs," p. 39)

Item	Size	Appearance	Use	Estimated Cost	Urgency (if found, buy at once, when affordable)

Seating
  sofa
  love seat
  upholstered
    chairs
  wood chairs
  other					

Sleeping
  sleep sofa
  bed(s)					

Tables
  dining
  coffee
  end
  bedside
  card
  others					

Flooring					
Lamps					
Accessories					

FILL-IN CHART: WHAT'S ON HAND

Item	Size	Present Use	Future Use	How to Redo	How to Replace	Urgency (if found, buy at once, when affordable)

Seating
  sofa
  love seat
  upholstered chairs
  wood chairs
  other						

Sleeping
  sleep sofa
  bed(s)						

Tables
  dining
  coffee
  end
  bedside
  card
  others						

Flooring						
Lamps						
Accessories						

4

Color, Texture, and Pattern

Although when we think of decorating we tend to think of furniture first, color, texture, and pattern have greater importance. These three design elements working together can hide a multitude of sins or point up desirable features. They are among the most important elements in creating the mood of a home — formal or informal, traditional or modern, welcoming or forbidding.

In this chapter, we will discuss each of these elements separately, but it is important to remember that they actually work together, and the total effect is what is important.

COLOR THEORY

What is color?

The basic definition of color is that it is the quality of light reflected to the eye. The light which is not absorbed by a surface is seen by us as color. When something appears to be red, it does so because all the other colors are absorbed by its surface, leaving only the red.

Definitions, while interesting, are not of much use when it comes to selecting colors to use for interiors. And ideas of how to use color in decorating are subject to fashion. Many rooms that had shock value when first decorated look out of date now because the ideas of color first used in those rooms have been overused in later years. Combinations of bright colors such as intense pink and strong orange were sensational when first used widely for rooms in the 1960's; today they are beginning to look dated.

Theories develop, are expounded, are seen as revealed truth, become widely accepted, and finally disappear. The eye is first startled by "new" colors, then accepting, eventually bored, and finally disdainful.

Color can date a room or a decorating scheme (and give a good clue to your own age) more quickly than almost any other element in your home, but color can usually be more easily and inexpensively changed than any other decorating element.

We mentioned that color ideas come and go in fashion. Depending on the mood of fashion itself, colors may either be rich, as in Victorian times, paled, as in the early days of modern furniture and decorating, or bright and primary, as in recent European-influenced interiors.

Today, we're moving back in the direction of the Victorian ideal while maintaining interest in the neutral colors of the modern movement.

COLD AND WARM

Over the years we've also seen changes in theories about how colors should be used. Blue, for instance, was once considered (and still is by many) a cold color, yellow a warm color. The terms *warm* and *cool* are used in describing colors in several senses. In addition to implying an impression of actual physical warmth, the word *warm* when used of a color also implies welcoming and friendly. The word *cool* used of colors means not only giving an impression of physical coolness but also has a suggestion of being less welcoming, perhaps even somewhat depressing. A room facing north, this theory held, should be painted yellow to warm it; a room facing south should be painted blue to cool it.

There is a degree of truth to the concept of warm and cool colors, although deep blues and blues with a hint of red are considered less cool than gray blues and very pale blues, and similar things can be said of other colors.

At one time it was also believed (and again still is to a certain extent) that pale colors extended space and dark colors made spaces appear smaller. This led to an infinite number of small apartments, bungalows (the forerunner of the ranch house), and other structures, including many public buildings, whose interiors were painted pale beige. This color became less popular, then boring, and became known as "apartment house tan" because it was used by so many landlords of apartment houses. Today it is returning as one of the "new" neutrals.

For years it was believed that more than one color shouldn't be used in decorating the very small house or apartment. Today, we're going back to a belief in many colors, to more use of wallpaper, to pattern-on-pattern.

Colors come in and go out of fashion on grounds of practicality, too. White is a perfect example of this. When the first all-white room was introduced it was considered revolutionary. The all-white room was either really all-white — walls, floor, furniture, even vases and flowers — or white with perhaps one or two accent colors. It was startling in the context of the color fashion period in which it was introduced, when many people were still in favor of the deeply colored Victorian look for decorating. More important, perhaps, the all-white room was considered impractical when it was first seen. A series of all-white rooms, however, has proved that this is not necessarily so. In time, an all-white color scheme became a signal of a certain fashion awareness.

Establishing your own color preferences takes time and effort, and this is where looking at pictures of rooms, seeing model rooms, and deciding what it is you like about a specific room can help.

RULES ON COLOR

Despite changing fashions in color theory and use, there are certain rules to be aware of — even if you break them. The point in knowing about rules in decorating, like any other craft, is that they have evolved because they work well in most situations. They have been tried over a period of time and usually are safe. Today, more and more decorators, individuals, and decorating publications, tired of safety, are urging the breaking of these rules. This is fine and can work well — provided you are aware when you break them that this is what you are doing.

Here are some basic color rules to follow or ignore.

• Cool colors such as blue, green, and violet make a room seem to recede, seem cooler, and make it seem more spacious. Cool colors should be used in rooms facing south, to cool them off.

• Warm colors advance. Warm colors include red, orange, and yellow. They make a room seem warmer and should be used in rooms facing north, to warm them up.

• Small houses and small apartments should be decorated in the same colors throughout. This way, the smallness is less claustrophobic and, when one room is glimpsed from another, the colors seem to merge into each other.

• No more than four colors should be used in one room — any more and the room appears confused and too busy.

• Window walls should be a lighter color than other walls. The window wall is the darkest wall; having it a lighter color minimizes this.

Breaking the Rules

Having listed those rules, we can think of a hundred places where they've been broken and the rooms have still looked right. Here are some examples of how they can be broken.

Blue is not always a cold color. There are warm blues — generally the darker ones, including navy. These colors warm up a room, particularly if the room has, for instance, navy blue walls picking up the deep blue in an oriental rug.

Rooms facing directly north are relatively rare. Then, too, the rule that warm colors must be used there assumes that the north side of a house or apartment will be perpetually cold, while the south side will be perpetually hot. A lot depends on how much light actually reaches a room. A lot depends on how much sunny weather there is where you live.

There's no point in trying to warm up a room facing north in a tropical or semi-tropical climate. There's no point in cooling down a room facing south in a chilly, rainy environment. Furthermore, the quality of sunlight changes as one moves nearer the equator and as we move from season to season.

Contrary to the rules on warm and cold colors, as we move nearer the equator the sun seems to wash color out of the cool colors. That's why such hot colors as vibrant pink and bright orange look right in the tropics. In theory, only the cool colors would work, but actually they look pale and indecisive under such light. That's why a fabric that seems just right in the tropics often looks garish in a temperate zone.

The main reason the color theories are no longer as important as they once were, however, is that they were developed for homes using natural light almost exclusively during daylight hours. Few of us do that today. In cities, we are too crowded together to manage it. Out of cities, unless we live in a glass house, we have found that natural light is inadequate for many of our daily tasks. The light we use in our homes is usually incandescent. This is close to sunlight but has slightly more red in it and it warms up even cold colors.

Today's Color Rules

Today's color rules are just as theoretical as those of the past, and just as arbitrary.

A world full of orange coffee shops should tell you that there is a belief that orange makes people hungrier. It probably does until too many experiences with bad food in an orange environment bring disillusionment.

Red is considered a good color to work with; it is also still somewhat avant garde as a wall color or floor color.

Despite trends toward neutral colorings and deep brown, and a fashion for contrasting colors, the main trend today is to more courage in color. The question, of course, is "What is courage?" The Victorian look using old rose and off-blue may be one person's color courage and another person's old hat.

INTRODUCING COLOR

Once you have worked out what colors you want for your home, how do you bring them into your decorating program?

Color can be introduced into a room in many ways. Paint is the least expensive way to use color. Even white paint makes a color statement in its strong contrast to any other color and because it works with any other color. Paint can be used on walls, used to pick out moldings and woodwork around doors, door frames, and windows, spread on the floor, put on the ceiling, put on wood furniture.

Fabric is another way of introducing color. Upholstered furniture is covered with fabric; rugs are usually fabric; curtains, too, make their own color statement in fabric. Fabric often, though not necessarily, includes the introduction of pattern, adding to the color mix.

Wallpaper should be considered at the same time as fabric, although there are no-color no-design wallpapers, such as the grass cloth wallpapers, which rely on texture for their statement. Most wallpapers, however, introduce both color and pattern to a room and, like fabric, make color schemes slightly more complicated.

Light is often overlooked in color scheme considerations, but it shouldn't be. The light cast through colored lamp shades affects the quality of the colors in the room and the colors in the room affect the quality of the light. See the section on lighting for more complete information. For now, keep in mind that the all-blue room, for instance, may need a softening light (perhaps a lamp with a red lamp shade) to keep people in the room from looking blue themselves from the reflected light.

CHOOSING A SCHEME

With all these things to consider, how does one ever hit on a color scheme?

Over the years, you've probably developed some feelings about color. You may like green, hate purple and lavender. You may think brown looks dirty, adore navy blue.

Focus these feelings before you start decorating by checking out what colors are already important in your own life (for clothes or whatever) and what colors seem right to you when you look at room interiors in stores or magazines.

Don't be surprised if your taste in clothing colors is different from your taste in decorating. Clothing color tastes are often determined by what looks well on you, decorating color tastes by what sets the mood you want. Both are likely to change over the years, partly because of fashion influences and partly because taste tends to change with experience.

Furniture no longer dictates your color scheme to the

same extent as it once did. You may feel happier, however, using the colors associated with the decorating period that corresponds to most of your furniture. Regency furniture, for instance, seems to work best with rich colors such as maroon and dark green. However, it also works well with bright gold, deep blue, and similar colors. Your furniture will probably adapt itself to whatever color schemes you like. Check the chart in chapter 5 for color ideas, and then make up your own mind.

One of the most effective ways to choose a color scheme is by making a list of your favorite colors. Then look for a fabric, wallpaper, or painting that uses some of those colors. Start with it to build your color scheme and go on from there.

These items, of course, have their own color schemes, which is why they can help you. If you use a printed fabric you may find as many as five colors in it. Use one for the floor, the fabric itself for the sofa and curtains, another color for the walls, and a third as an accent.

Using a fabric has another advantage, one you don't have if you use a painting. Fabric designers do not exist in a vacuum. The colors they use are colors which will be found in other decorating items, including rugs and paints. This can make your decorating much easier and faster.

How Many Colors?

How many colors can you use in one room? It's generally agreed that you can deliberately introduce as many as four colors into a room and it will still work, but since most of us own things in colors that aren't part of our basic scheme, keeping to only three deliberately introduced colors is a good idea. Black and white usually don't count unless they are used in large enough quantities to become colors in themselves, as when a white sofa is set against a black rug.

Although wood finishes are, of course, different colors, from the red tones of some maple finishes to the grayed tones of some ash finishes, they are usually not considered colors in planning schemes. The only time they are is when they are violently contrasting, as when a room contains about equal amounts of a very red finish and a very yellow finish, for instance. In such a case, it is usually a good idea to restain some of the furniture so the contrast is less.

Once you've worked out which are your basic three colors, start looking for things in those colors. If you've chosen colors you really like you'll find yourself pouncing when you see anything from a wastebasket to a lamp in one of your room's colorings. Gradually, the dominant colors in the room will come to be the ones you have chosen.

Handling Color Schemes

There are certain basic principles in working with color schemes. Again, these are rules that can be followed or ignored. The important thing is to know that they exist.

• Contrasting color schemes are easier to work with than monochromatic schemes. This is because monochromatic schemes can prove both dull and depressing unless the contrast lacking in the colors is provided by texture or pattern. In working with colors, a color wheel is often used for inspiration. It is a rainbow arranged in a circle.

• A contrasting scheme uses colors which are distant from each other on a color wheel. A monochromatic color scheme uses either the same color throughout or colors which are very close to each other on the color wheel. Contrasting color scheme possibilities include red, white, and blue, for instance. Monochromatic color schemes include all blue or, possibly, dark blue, lavender, and light blue.

• In contemporary decorating, the monochromatic scheme represented by neutral colors close to the wood tones of the natural, dull-finish wood furniture is most popular.

• A third type of color scheme, often called a complementary scheme, can also be very successful. For this scheme, two contrasting colors are used, accented by another version of one of the two colors. An orange, yellow, green scheme, for instance, falls into this category. It could be created with a leaf green rug, orange, yellow, and green flowered draperies, yellow and orange stripes on the sofa, and light yellow walls.

COLOR TRICKS

There are certain tricks to using color that don't qualify as rules but are good to know.

• If you have deeply set windows, paint the inside of the frame a light blue. This seems to bring the sky into your home.

• If you have a very high ceiling and want to lower it (you may not want to), painting it or papering it in any contrasting color will seem to do so. This is especially effective if it repeats the color of the rug.

• Color can highlight or obscure architectural detailings. Although during the white-for-everything era white doors, windows frames, and moldings were the rule, today we're more likely to paint them in at least two colors to accent the detail. If you dislike the moldings, painting them the same color as the wall will obscure them. The darker the color of the wall they match the more they will seem to disappear.

TEXTURE

Equally as important as color, although not as dramatic in its immediate impact, is texture. Texture refers to the tactile

sense — touch — but we experience texture not only through our skin but also through our eyes. Color, on the other hand, we only experience through our eyes.

Texture can be divided into certain categories. These include:

> smooth, as in a very shiny lacquered surface;
> rough, as in a brick wall;
> fluffy, as in a shaggy rug;
> soft, as in a mohair blanket;
> hard, as in a piece of wood.

Within these groupings there can be variations. A single fabric can, for instance, combine both fluffy and smooth yarns. A rough wall (brick, for instance) can be covered with a smooth (enamel) paint.

Texture is important because it adds an additional dimension to a room. Occasionally, a room will be deliberately decorated entirely in one texture but this gives a certain dullness. Extremely clinical kitchens, for instance, may be furnished with nothing but shiny surfaces for easy cleaning. Such a room benefits from some contrasting texture such as a brick wall to relieve its sterility.

THE MONOCHROME ROOM

The popular monochrome neutral room — using, for instance, only tones of earth color — also needs textural relief. Such a room is most successful when it combines, for example, the hardness of a natural-stained wood table with a smooth and fluffy neutral-colored fabric covering the sofa with a soft neutral-colored rug.

Rooms with a monochromatic color scheme, such as all-blue rooms, also need textural relief. The all-white rooms of the past were only successful when textural contrast provided interest. Otherwise these rooms become boring and eventually rather depressing.

We have talked here so much about the importance of texture that we have left out a warning. There is a danger with texture. Too many textures, like too many colors, can give a room an uneasy, nervous quality. Probably it's best if, in a contrasting room, no more than three textures are introduced. For the monochromatic room, as many as five different textures can work well, but three is still safer.

PATTERN

Pattern can be as important as color and texture, although not every room uses pattern or needs pattern. It should be taken into consideration in your decorating plans so that whether you omit it or use it you make a deliberate decision.

Today, pattern is much more widely available than it was. There are wall patterns (wallpaper), floor patterns (rugs, tiling), and, of course, fabric patterns. At one time, pattern was used sparingly. Only one pattern was used to a room, so that if your walls had wallpaper with a pattern, your furniture would be either plain colored or, at most, covered with a striped fabric. Today, we are in a period of mixed pattern use which hasn't been equalled since Victorian times; pattern is being used with pattern with different designs combined and contrasted.

Here are a few rules that most experts follow in using pattern. Like all rules in this book, they are given so that you will know about them, even if you decide to break them.

• Patterns used in the same room should be united in color. Combinations of pattern seem to work best when the same colors are repeated — a floral pattern in orange, yellow, and green works best with a plaid in the same orange, yellow, and green, perhaps with another geometric orange, yellow, and green pattern added.

• The scale of the patterns used together is important, too. Too much of a large splashy pattern tends to overpower a room. The addition of another large splashy pattern turns such a room into a disaster area. Small-scale patterns seem to work together better than large-scale patterns.

• Pattern, like color, changes its effect when used in quantity. Unless you are very sure — and perhaps even then — look at a large sample of a pattern in the room where you plan to use it, and look at it with samples of the other patterns or colors you plan to use. Don't just look at it for five minutes, either. Leave it out in the room so that you can see it without expecting to see it. This will have a surprise element which will give you a better impression of how it actually looks.

• Patterns usually have some degree of regularity to them so that in quantity (as on a sofa, in curtains, on a wall) there are definite vertical, horizontal, or diagonal lines. Look at a large enough piece of the pattern you are considering to determine if the repetition it has (called rhythm) will annoy you.

• Stripes, checks, and plaids are usually considered pattern. They are generally a little easier to work with than other patterns, although perhaps not as interesting.

• The smaller the pattern the more likely it is to blend into itself from a distance. It is important to view all patterns from a distance. Red, white, and blue, for example, in a small enough scale, will appear to be a rather peculiar purple.

• In using more than one pattern in a room, be sure that each pattern is used in large enough quantity to stand out. If, for instance, you cover the sofa with a large, splashy floral chintz and pick the colors of the chintz up with a plaid, the plaid (which will give the appearance of being more subtle than the floral print) should be used on at least two chairs in the room. The chairs themselves don't have to be matching — just the fabric.

• Pattern on the floor is a newly popular trend thanks largely to the interest in rya and Oriental rugs. If you use patterned rugs, the other items in the room should pick up the colors of the rug in the same way as the plaid in the example above reflects the color of the print. Otherwise, the effect is that the rug is "fighting" the rest of the room.

SEEING A ROOM

The best way to be sure the various elements of a room will work together is to try to "see" it before you are finally committed to it. Decorators swatch (take small pieces of) fabrics and rugs they plan to use and attach them to paper to keep all the elements of a room together. Paint samples and wallpaper samples go there, too. If you follow this system, you can see all the color, texture, and pattern elements of your room together and judge whether they mix or fight.

Such a sheet is useful in another way, too. It is almost impossible to remember colors in your head. If you have your samples with you when you shop, you can check immediately to see if colors are right.

The chart which follows can be copied for as many rooms as you are decorating. If you are planning to keep certain elements in the room the same as they are now — which is the way most of us decorate — be sure to include them in your chart. These charts are designed to be filled in with words but can also be swatched.

SAMPLE CHART OF POSSIBLE COLOR, TEXTURE, AND PATTERN SCHEMES

Item	Color(s)	Texture	Pattern
Wood furniture	Painted blue drawers; white trimming	Smooth	None
Flooring	Covered by rug	None	None
Rug	Blue	Fluffy (shag)	None
Sofa	Red, white, blue chintz	Smooth	Crewel-like floral print
Chair 1	Red and white stripes	Smooth	Striped
Chair 2	Red and white stripes	Smooth	Striped
Chair 3			
Chair 4			
Walls	White	Rough	None
Ceiling	Blue of furniture	Rough	None
Blind	White venetian	Smooth	None
Shade			
Curtains			
Draperies	Same chintz as sofa	Smooth	Crewel-like floral print
Bed(s)			

FILL-IN CHART:
COLOR, TEXTURE, AND PATTERN SCHEMES

Item	Color(s)	Texture	Pattern
Wood furniture			
Flooring			
Rug			
Sofa			
Chair 1			
Chair 2			
Chair 3			
Chair 4			
Walls			
Ceiling			
Blind			
Shade			
Curtains			
Draperies			
Bed(s)			

5

What Is Period Furniture?

One thing that makes many people nervous about decorating is talk about furnishing in a specific period. People will ask, "Is your home modern?" or "Is your home French provincial?" to the point where you'll wonder if Early Marriage can be a home at all.

The term *period furnishing* refers primarily to the furniture styles themselves. There were specific furniture styles in most historical periods. To be truly authentic, a room would have to be furnished in antiques or, if the room is modern or contemporary, in original designs by the first designer who thought of a furniture design. Most truly authentic rooms have ended up in museums, which is why you won't see them around your neighborhood.

However, because of the common use of these terms and because they are a shorthand way of describing the look you want, this chapter is a discussion of period furniture. In addition, at the end of the chapter there is a chart showing what each period was noted for and what some of the current names are for each period.

CLASS DISTINCTIONS

You have to realize, first of all, that until recently class distinctions were reflected in furniture design. By looking at the kind of furniture people had you could tell how rich they were and what their position in life was. This is still true to a certain extent — after all, the best of modern design is extremely expensive — but because the ideal of modern decorating at its most advanced is one of utter simplicity and bareness, the differences aren't as apparent.

In the past, most people had little furniture in the sense that we think of it. They had chairs, chests of drawers, beds, and tables, made either by family members from available wood or by local carpenters, but there was no furniture industry until the late 1800's.

The royal courts in Europe set the styles for furniture as they set the styles for everything else. And, because the courts were seats of wealth and practical considerations (such as dusting) were attended to by numerous servants, court furniture was very elaborate. Outside court circles, people who wanted to show they were up-to-date would have furniture made up by local carpenters in the styles of the great court furniture makers. This furniture was usually less formal, perhaps less well made, often more comfortable. It was either left in the natural wood or painted — court furniture, however, was likely to be gilded. If you like the look of antique French furniture, for example, but feel it's a little stiff for your life, you might prefer what is now called French provincial. The styles which developed away from the courts are usually given names such as *provincial, country,* or *rustic,* to indicate that they reflect life away from the life of the court.

The distinction between one class and another held true even in the United States. The furniture that you see in Williamsburg, Virginia, for instance, is actually English William and Mary and Queen Anne furniture. These pieces were usually imported from England for a limited number of wealthy people in what were then the colonies. Early American furniture — the type of furniture most people had and used — is much more crudely made; it was made by local carpenters or family members.

FASHION IN FURNITURE

Fashion was and is a part of furniture design just as it is of clothing, and fashions in one area affect fashions in other areas. Today's furniture, which at its most advanced may consist only of big cushions covered with fabric, reflects the belief of many people in contemporary society that objects don't matter, sitting "properly" doesn't matter, and comfort is all.

Because of the isolation of one country from another and the lack of rapid communication such as we have today, the courts of Europe tended to be very much on their own. That is why different styles of furniture emerged — from the heavy look of Spanish furniture to the light look of French furniture (gilding emphasized the lightness even more) to the solid look of English court furniture.

Shaker furniture is another American furniture style which is often considered to belong to the colonial period. Actually, although the lines are somewhat similar, this furniture was developed in the nineteenth century by an ascetic religious group with several communities in the United States. The group designed many simple styles of furniture so that the time saved from cleaning could be spent in prayer.

MODERN FURNITURE

"Modern" or "contemporary" is a furniture look we all know, but it is hard to define. It can range from the delightful to the appalling, depending on whether it was well designed or just thrown together. This furniture was originally extremely austere — that clinical look of the early part of this century is an example. Some pieces have become classics.

Perhaps the best-known modern piece of furniture is the plastic shell chair which, copied and copied, has become a cliché of airport waiting rooms. The original plastic shell chair has a seat which is so shaped that it hugs and supports figures of almost any size and people of almost any age. Many of the copies have been made smaller and less contoured, eliminating much of the comfort of the original.

Wood is extremely important in contemporary furniture

design, whether used in a big slab for a desk or coffee table and finished with a dull sheen, or molded. Molded wood, including plywood, predates the use of molded plastic and probably inspired plastic contoured (shaped to the body) furniture.

ECLECTIC DECORATING

It is hard to tell what present trends, if any, will continue to appeal to future generations, and we should remember that what one generation hates is often appreciated by the next. We're now in a multi-faceted decorating period which magazines and decorators call *eclectic*, which in this sense simply means that anything can be used with anything else. It's a reaction against the old theory that only early American furniture could be used with early American furniture and that if you added a modern coffee table, you ruined the entire look.

The idea of eclectic styling isn't new; its acceptance by taste makers is, however. Several styles have always existed side by side, so that the stark modern of the early part of this century existed side by side with more decorated styles.

MASS PRODUCTION

During the nineteenth and twentieth centuries, period furniture of other times became highly respected. Part of the basis for this respect was a reaction against mass production. As with all new products, mass-produced furniture had its growing pains, and many influential people sneered at the results of mass production. This sneering continues.

If you are familiar with the furniture available from mass producers today you may wonder why we have bothered to discuss period furniture at all. Mass-produced furniture today, although it almost always bows in the direction of one or another definite style, is a hodgepodge of divergent influences, including the ideals of the furniture designer and the exigencies of the mass production method.

Most of us buy furniture made by a mass producer. At its worst, this furniture may be tasteless, poorly proportioned, or reflect an attempt to imitate expensive furniture of the past with shoddy materials and construction. At its best — not necessarily its most expensive — this furniture can be excellent. It often combines the best of the past and present (wood, for instance, for appearance and detail, plastic for easy care) and is often scaled to fit contemporary rooms, usually smaller than those in which the furniture was originally used.

PERIOD FURNITURE

Baroque

Tudor

Elizabethan

Jacobean

Louis XIV

William and Mary

PERIOD FURNITURE

Early American

French provincial

Windsor chair

Joint stool

Queen Anne

Régence

Chinese Chippendale

Ribband Back Chippendale

Eighteenth-century American

PERIOD FURNITURE

Louis XV

Rococo

Louis XVI

Empire

Directoire

Regency

Federal

PERIOD FURNITURE

Biedermeier

Victorian

Mission

Shaker

Barcelona chair

Plastic chair

PERIOD FURNISHINGS CHART

Year	Italy	France	England	Americas	Other	Modern Adaptations by Furniture Industry
1550 on	Baroque: irregular, asymmetrical; marble, wood, plaster; brilliant colors		Tudor, Elizabethan, Jacobean: heavy, regular forms; dark wood, often oak; crimson	Some Spanish, notably in missions: heavy; dark wood; similar to Tudor	Spanish (see Americas)	Usually given name of period, as Tudor, Baroque
1650		Louis XIV (reigned 1643–1715): large, majestic, decorated, linear; used marble, wood, plastic; green, crimson, gold, blue; stylized sun used as symbol				Mediterranean
1700			William & Mary (reigned, 1689–1702): both straight and curved lines; walnut; pale colors or bright prints with white; secretaries, cabinets developed Queen Anne (reigned 1702–1714): curved lines; walnut, then mahogany; blues, greens; upholstered sofas; Oriental influence		Colonial, early American copies of English court styles; native woods, notably pine; wealthy followed English styles, often ten or fifteen years later	Both French provincial and Italian provincial styles are adaptations of court furniture: Italian is relatively linear, French is relatively curved; fruitwoods and fruitwood finishes Early American adaptations are the best-selling furniture style in the United States

PERIOD FURNISHINGS CHART

Year	Italy	France	England	Americas	Other	Modern Adaptations by Furniture Industry
1715		Régence (1715–1723): less regular forms	Georgian (1714–1810): heavy columned pieces; mahogany, highly polished; ingenious, versatile tables; many styles originated by furniture makers such as Chippendale, Hepplewhite, and Sheraton			Georgian adaptations are often called either eighteenth-century English or, simply, traditional
1720 1750	Rococo (1720-1760): similar to Baroque; flower, ribbon, shell designs; ITALIAN INFLUENCE DECLINES	Louis XV (reigned 1723–1774): light, asymmetrical, curved, small scale; gold decoration on wood; pale pastels plus white and gold; chinoiserie				
1775		Louis XVI (reigned 1774–1789): straight lines, geometric forms, columns; prints, stripes, gray; classical influence				

PERIOD FURNISHINGS CHART

Year	Italy	France	England	Americas	Other	Modern Adaptions by Furniture Industry
1800		Directoire (1795–1804): less decorated; light-colored wood plus ebony, mahogany; red, white, blue; drums, spears as accents Empire (1804–1814): symmetrical, heavy; wine, yellow, purple; wallpaper classical influence; initial N (for Napoleon) used as accent FRENCH INFLUENCE DECLINES	Regency (1810–1820): continued classical influence; cane; light green, deep green, beige, dark brown, crimson, yellow, purple, stripes; many tables; Oriental influence strong	Federal (1780–1825): classical, curved legs; mahogany; olive green, blue, gray, red, white; eagle decorations	Biedermeier (Germany): comfortable, inexpensive, occasionally clumsy; black lacquer, multi-color painted peasantlike decorations	Adaptations may be called Regency, Empire, or simply traditional
1820			Victorian (Victoria reigned 1837-1901): rococo, Gothic revived; rosewood, mahogany; mauve, purple, red, green, gold; carved fruit, flowers; period of Industrial Revolution and development of mass-produced furniture	Victorian: ornate, pointed arches mahogany, rosewood, marble tops, rich colors as in England		Victorian adaptations widely available
1835				Shaker: developed at same time; simple lines, usually straight; native wood, often pine; ingenious solutions for storage, such as wall pegs		Shaker styling, despite dates of its development, is usually adapted and included as a part of early American

6
Buying Wood Furniture

Wood is one of the oldest and most commonly used materials for making furniture. It is plentiful in most areas of the world and from earliest times has been valued because of its versatility and practicality. Wood can be stained, painted, carved, cut, bent under heat, and glued. The development of veneering (laminating) techniques means that an inferior wood can be covered with a thin veneer (layer) of another wood, achieving more attractive grain patterns.

Possibly because of our interest in handcrafted antiques, possibly for other reasons, more has been written in books and magazines about buying wood furniture than about most other items for the home. Many standards established for buying wood furniture are almost impossible to realize. They are good ideals, but because in many cases the furniture industry no longer follows the techniques upon which these ideals were based, they are impractical. In this book, therefore, we will tell you what the ideal standards are but alert you to the fact that wood furniture meeting these standards may be difficult or impossible to find.

COMMON TERMS

Wood furniture has its own language. To understand what you are buying you should be familiar with the most commonly used terms and their meanings. Here is a listing of some of them.

• *Case goods* is the term by which the furniture industry refers to wooden furniture. It probably came originally from wooden "cases," such as chests of drawers, but is now extended to all wood furniture, including chairs and tables.

• *Solid* used with the name of a wood means that all exposed wood (the wood you can see) is actually the wood named. *Solid maple* means that the top, sides, and front of a piece are made of maple — but the rest of the piece can be made from another material, including, for instance, plastic or fiberboard. Solid wood has no veneer.

• *Veneer* is made of thin layers of wood permanently joined together. These layers are usually bonded at right angles to each other. The top layer, also called the veneer, is a wood with an attractive grain. The word *laminated* is occasionally used instead of *veneered*.

• *Grain* in wood refers to the pattern formed by the tissues which make up the wood. Determining what is an attractive grain is an extremely subjective process.

• *Genuine*, as in *genuine mahogany*, usually means that the exposed parts are veneer.

• *Combination* is used to describe furniture in which more than one type of wood is used for the exposed parts. For instance, genuine walnut veneer might be used for the front in combination with another solid wood for the other exposed parts.

• *All-wood construction* means that the parts of the wood you see are wood throughout the entire thickness of the piece. Some furniture is made with hollow sections (on the front, for instance) to save money or reduce weight; that is not all-wood construction. You can check this point by rapping on the wood. If it sounds hollow, it is. All-wood furniture has a dull sound when knocked.

The point in defining these terms isn't that one type of

construction is necessarily better than the other, but that the terms can be misleading. It helps to know what they mean.

There are advantages and disadvantages to the various types of construction. Solid wood, because it is the same throughout the exposed parts, is easier to repair or refinish. There are no layers at the edges, and since there is no veneer, there is no chance that the veneer can become loose or chip off.

Veneer furniture, on the other hand, has strength with lightness and resists warping and swelling because of the way the grains of the layers cross each other. Furthermore, the use of veneer makes it possible for a relatively weak wood with a beautiful grain or color to be used with a firmer wood to make a piece of furniture that has the advantages of both.

HARDWOOD AND SOFTWOOD

There are two other confusing terms used in the furniture industry — *hardwood* and *softwood*. These terms have nothing to do with how hard or how soft the woods are, although oak is often used as an example of a hardwood and pine as an example of a softwood. Hardwoods are woods from deciduous trees — trees that lose their leaves every year in temperate zones. Softwoods are evergreens (including redwood, a pretty sturdy wood).

Certain types of wood are better for certain types of furniture than other woods. Dense woods, such as ash, poplar, and the very important gum, are used for the frames of furniture and interior parts that have to be strong, stable, and able to take shocks. Gumwood is much maligned, so maligned, in fact, that even its name is rarely used. It is usually referred to as "American hardwood." Several trees used for furniture are given the name *gum*. The one most commonly used for American-made furniture is the sweet or red gum. The wood from this tree is sometimes called sap gum. Less commonly used gumwoods which are, however, extremely important in furniture making belong to the Nyssa family. These are the water tupelo and the black tupelo. Gumwood is extremely strong, plentiful, and excellent for its purpose. As its grain is not considered attractive, it is used with a veneer most of the time.

WOOD AND DESIGN

Certain types of furniture design demand certain types of wood for their construction. The rocker part of rocking chairs, for instance, is most often made of maple, beech, or birch. This is because these woods are dense and therefore strong. Solid pine is often used to make copies of early American furniture, as it was often used for the originals and can be carved and colored in the same way.

Because of their beauty, woods such as birch, cherry, mahogany, oak, pecan, and walnut are used for furniture whose exteriors must be able to take a good-looking finish and a polish. These woods are used either as solid woods or as veneer.

Certain woods are considered exotic. There include teak, rosewood, and ebony. They are usually considered exotic both because of their coloring and because of the beauty of their grains. None of these woods grows in the United States in quantity. They are used almost entirely as veneers or for small areas of decoration on other woods.

Veneer, although somewhat frowned upon in the past because inferior veneer can separate from its backing, has many advantages over solid wood. Veneers can be matched and arranged to form a pattern in a way which is almost impossible in the solid woods. Higher standards and improvements in the methods of making veneer furniture have eliminated many of the former objections to its use.

Most fine wood furniture today (fine in this instance also implies expensive) is made of either solid wood or veneer. About 90 percent of the furniture made by mass producers is veneered.

RECONSTITUTED WOODS

Various "reconstituted" woods are also used in furniture manufacture. These include hardboard, particle board, wood chip, and plywood.

Hardboard is made of small fibers of wood which are pressed together under heat. It looks like regular wood when finished but is stronger and more resistant to moisture than many other woods. *Wood chip* is made in a similar way. *Particle board* is made of a combination of wood flakes and resins which are pressed into sheets and then usually covered with veneer. *Plywood* is made of layers of wood joined together so that the grains are at right angles. This makes a stronger wood for its thickness than would be obtainable otherwise. Plywood can be molded under heat more effectively than most woods.

Relatively few pieces of wood furniture commercially available today are made entirely of wood. You will find furniture made of molded plastic combined with wood, furniture with plastic veneer made to resemble wood, and real wood with an artificial grain.

In many cases, such things as drawer glides and other small components of wood furniture may be made of plastic, simply because plastic has proved to be more practical (either in terms of money or in terms of durability) than wood.

THE JOINTS

One of the classic ways in which the quality of wood furniture can be judged is the way in which the various parts are joined together. New materials — and especially the synthetic adhesives — have changed some of the old rules.

Furniture is joined by adhesives, screws, nails, and joints. In most cases, you won't find all these joining methods in one piece of furniture.

The adhesive chosen is extremely important. Old-fashioned glues tended to dry out, resulting in wobbly joints. Modern synthetic adhesives do not have this failing, but some experts feel they are too rigid for use in joints (such as chair legs) that need to move somewhat to avoid breaking the wood.

Areas of wood furniture which must be able to move or expand and contract are best joined together with a combination of adhesive and screws. In high-quality furniture, the holes left by the screws are filled with plastic wood or putty. This kind of furniture rarely contains nails.

The joints themselves can be classified according to strength.

JOINTS

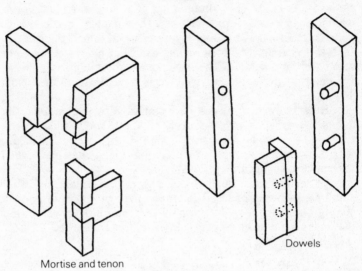

Mortise and tenon

Dowels

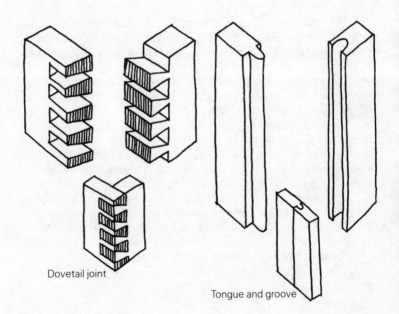

Dovetail joint

Tongue and groove

JOINTS

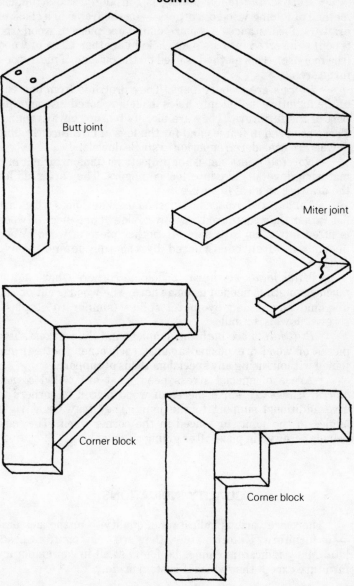

Butt joint

Miter joint

Corner block

Corner block

• *Mortise and tenon* joining is considered the strongest method of joining wood at corners — on the frame of a chest of drawers, for instance. A square end of one piece of wood (the tenon) is inserted into a square hole in another piece of wood (the mortise). This method is used on the outside of most wood furniture.

• *Dowels* are wooden pegs. They protrude from one end of the furniture and fit into holes drilled or bored into another part of the furniture. They are usually but not always round. These are used in frames and for the legs of furniture. Double dowels are considered superior to single dowels.

• *Dovetail joints* consist of projections (pins) which fit into matching dovetails like interlocked fingers. They are used for the drawers on most furniture.

• *Tongue and groove* is a method used for joints which are flat rather than contoured. A convex side of one piece of wood is fitted into a concave side of another piece of wood. Wood flooring is often constructed by the tongue-and-groove method.

• *Miter joints* are a way of joining corners where not as much strength is needed as elsewhere. The wood is cut on the diagonal and joined by metal spikes (similar to staples), screws, dowels, or nails.

• *Butt joints* are both the simplest and the weakest. Two pieces of wood are pushed against each other (butted) and joined without using any special methods of support.

• Areas of special stress need what are called *corner blocks*. These are small pieces of wood placed in corners to give additional support to the joint. They may be at right angles to the joint, or placed in the corner itself. They are usually screwed in place after gluing and notching.

QUALITY INDICATIONS

There are various indicators of quality — or the lack of it — in furniture. Unfortunately, they are very far from absolute. Many indicators cannot be found at all in contemporary furniture except that which is custom made.

On large pieces of furniture, look at the back. Things to consider are whether or not it is of the same wood as the front. This is important if you plan to use the piece as a room divider, although, of course, you can always cover the back. The finish on the back of a high-quality piece of furniture should be as carefully applied as the one on the front. The back panel should be set into the frame of the back and screwed in place. In cheaper furniture the back is stapled on.

Test furniture with drawers by pulling them out. If they wobble or stick, the drawers are not right for that piece of furniture. There should be about a quarter inch of wiggle room around the drawers.

Side or center glides which support the drawers will be found in fine furniture. They make it easier to pull the drawers in and out and give the entire piece of furniture additional support. "Stops" are designed to keep the drawer from falling out of the drawer case. You should be able to overrule the stops fairly easily.

The best furniture has dust panels between the drawers. These are pieces of wood which keep dust out of the drawers and keep things from one drawer from being caught in another. Dust panels are an example of an ideal in furniture construction which is rarely found.

The best drawers have dovetail joints at all four corners and a drawer bottom that is joined into a groove on the sides and supported with corner blocks. These two features are also things you may have to compromise on.

The best furniture is joined with adhesive and screws, with the top of the screw covered by plastic wood or putty so it is almost impossible to see. Again, this is a construction feature you may find yourself having to give up.

The characteristics of doors on wood furniture are another indication of quality. Swinging doors should have a tendency to swing shut. The hinges should prevent the doors from sagging when open. Magnetic catches at top and bottom of the doors are a plus. Sliding doors should fit smoothly into their grooves which, ideally, should be cut into the furniture itself rather than being metal grooves attached later.

Check the hardware on all furniture. Look for solid hardware firmly attached. Although hardware is one of the easiest things to change on furniture if you don't like what the manufacturer has supplied, good original hardware is an indication of quality.

Hinges on furniture should be strong enough to do the work they are meant for. Hinges on swinging-door cabinets, for example, should keep the doors from sagging when open.

Tables should have certain features, too. Ideally they should be strong enough to stand on. This means legs which are well joined, with corner blocks reinforcing the corners. You should be able to push down on the table with most of your weight without making it sway.

Drop leaf tables and desks should work easily and have a hinge that locks in place. They are most satisfactory when supported by a collapsible leg. Otherwise, it is too easy to break off the leaf by leaning on it. An extension table, also called an expansion table (the kind with separate pieces of wood, called leaves, to make it larger) should be easily opened by one person. The table should not sag when all the leaves are in.

Glass used in furniture—as in china closets—should be clear, without flaws, unless deliberately flawed glass is used to give an antique effect.

The legs of all furniture pieces should be even so the piece doesn't wobble. Since floors aren't always even, self-leveling casters are a plus; they are found on the best furniture.

THE FINISH

The finish is one of the things which makes furniture expensive. Finishing is the final step in making wood furniture. Strictly speaking, the word *finish* is applied to wood, but laminated plastic and other synthetic materials also serve as finishes.

The first step in finishing furniture is sanding. Check such areas as the insides of drawers, the undersides of tables, chair seats, and legs. If these are rough, the sanding has been inadequate.

The next step in finishing is often staining. Uneven application of the stain causes obvious light or dark spots.

Check the finish (the very top of the wood). Lines across

the grain (called checking), an all-over pattern of cracks (called crazing), bubbles, streaks, and a rough surface are indications of poor finishing, and pieces with any of these problems should be rejected. If you order furniture from a floor sample and the pieces are delivered with any of these faults, return them. Since you are paying for a good finish on your furniture, you should get your money's worth. In buying an extension table, be sure the finish on the leaves is the same as the rest of the table.

TYPES OF FINISH

There are various types of finish, ranging from hand waxed to painted. A description of some types of finish follows.

• *Paint and lacquer* form a film on wood. Both clean easily, but if they are damaged are difficult to repair without either removing the surface entirely or leaving a mark. This group includes the extra-hard synthetic finishes such as polyurethanes. These may add to the price but are often worth buying for the protection they give to such things as tables that get a lot of use or abuse. On the other hand, these synthetic finishes have an almost glassy quality which may make them unappealing to some people. This group also includes the high-gloss finish popular for eighteenth-century furniture. Unless made with one of the synthetics, this finish is easily marred by water and alcohol and may tend to crack, craze, or bloom (look foggy) as humidity changes.

The finishes used in furniture being made today, including the high-gloss finishes, seal the wood so it does not require "feeding."

• An *oil finish*, also called a *natural finish*, has been popular for many years. It is duller than the lacquer type finishes and is especially popular on light woods, country styles, and some of the darker woods such as teak. An oil finish should be renewed by re-oiling every six months or so. You can either use your own mixture of 50 percent boiled linseed oil/50 percent alcohol or buy a similar oil already mixed.

Oil finishes are not as affected by water, alcohol, and humidity as the glossier finishes and when they are marred can usually be repaired by re-oiling. Many people feel that these finishes keep more of the natural look of the wood than the harder finishes do. Because the pores of the wood are not sealed by these finishes, the wood must be "fed" by application of either furniture polish or oil to avoid drying.

• A *distressed finish*, also called an *antique finish*, is a finish which looks as if it's been through the wars. Distressed finishes, which occasionally are found under the hard synthetic finishes, make the most sense when they are used with a natural finish. Distressing involves dents, marks, and spatters deliberately applied to the furniture. Don't make the mistake of thinking that a piece of distressed furniture is actually an antique.

• *Stains* are used to bring out the natural grain of a piece of wood, usually by darkening it. They are also used to imitate by their coloring the look of other woods or to give a different effect to a wood. They penetrate the wood and often change its color, but do not permanently seal it. Stained furniture should be labeled so that you'll know what you're getting, since very different effects can be obtained by putting a cherry, walnut, or maple finish on birch. The label should read "cherry-finished birch."

• Vinyl, though not actually a finish, is used as a finish on some pieces of furniture. A wood veneer or a photograph of the wood might be laminated to the vinyl.

• Melamine plastic (Formica, a trademark of American Cyanamid, is one) is also used in furniture. It can be colored or made to look like wood. This is especially popular for counter tops, even though it cracks under heat and is almost impossible to repair.

UNFINISHED FURNITURE

Unfinished furniture, also called unpainted furniture, has become more and more popular recently, both because there are great savings in buying unfinished furniture and because the quality of unfinished furniture has improved tremendously in recent years.

At one time unfinished furniture tended to be both shoddy and lacking in imagination. The styles of unpainted furniture now available range from modern to copies of eighteenth-century English and early American styles. Many sellers of unpainted furniture will finish the pieces if you prefer, but this may almost double the price.

It may be difficult to find attractive unfinished furniture in conventional department and furniture stores. Check to see if there is a store specializing in unpainted furniture in your neighborhood. Some lumberyards and home centers carry unpainted furniture.

Some of the best unfinished furniture is available from specialists by mail order. These companies advertise in decorating and general interest magazines. Many of these companies offer this furniture either finished or unfinished. If you order the furniture finished, you usually also receive a choice of stain or paint colors.

The same standards for judging any piece of wood furniture should be applied to unfinished furniture. You may be pleasantly surprised—this furniture is often better made than much already finished furniture. Furthermore, there are likely to be various custom options available at reasonable prices, such as plastic or wood tops, sliding wood or glass doors.

CARING FOR WOOD FURNITURE

How your wood furniture should be cared for is determined by the finish. Many traditional methods of care are not necessary with the new finishes. Of course, if you have an older piece of furniture (made before about 1960) you will use traditional methods, also listed below.

• *Paint, synthetic lacquer, plastic finishes.* Periodic dusting and occasional washing using soap suds (preferably not a detergent, which may react badly with the finish) on a sponge, followed by wiping with clear water and immediate, thorough drying are sufficient for this furniture

If you feel you must use a furniture wax or polish, don't risk using one which doesn't say "safe for painted surfaces." As these finishes seal the pores of the wood, feeding is not needed to prevent the wood from drying out or warping.

• *Glossy, non-synthetic finishes.* These are found on older pieces (before about 1960). In most cases, dusting and, if necessary, buffing (hard rubbing) is sufficient general care for this furniture. Use furniture polish or wax about once every six months; more frequent use may cause a dull film on the surface of the furniture. Avoid waxes containing silicones. These, although they give a greater shine, may prove abrasive.

Apply polish or wax sparingly, buff thoroughly, using a soft cloth. Any cloth used for buffing should be washed before the first use to remove any finishing materials that may have been used by the fabric manufacturer and which may scratch or stick to the polish or wax. Wipe up any spills that occur on this furniture quickly, and buff; if a stain remains, repolish.

• *Oil or natural finishes.* Although these finishes do not seal the wood, follow the instructions above. You may want to apply polish or wax more often than every six months, but to prevent discoloration from wax buildup avoid applying it more than four times a year. If the furniture appears very dirty (these finishes sometimes seem to hold dirt more than others) wash with a mild soap (not detergent) following the method described for painted finishes, then apply polish, oil, or wax.

• If you decide to use a wax rather than a furniture polish, be sure it is suitable for furniture. Certain floor waxes (usually the self-polishing type) contain chemicals which can destroy some furniture finishes.

Occasionally, if you change from one brand of furniture polish or wax to another, you may find a cloudy film forming with the first application. Use additional polish to remove the old polish.

If the polish or wax builds up to the point where it dulls the finish, you will have to remove it by using the soap and water method outlined above.

STAINS AND SCRATCHES

Most stains can be removed from the newer furniture finishes (and sometimes from the older) by simply buffing or by repolishing or waxing followed by buffing. Some softer finishes, however, are affected by water and alcohol.

If a water or alcohol (including perfume) stain doesn't

respond to buffing and repolishing or waxing, check the stain chart at the end of this section for possible ways to remove it. The chart lists traditional methods of removing stains from traditional, high-gloss furniture. Very deep stains should be either ignored, recolored (as in scratches, below), or sent to a professional refinisher.

Scratches can be ignored or filled in depending upon the kind of furniture. A scratch on an early American reproduction or a piece of furniture with a distressed finish is relatively unimportant; it simply adds to the appearance. A scratch on a more formally finished piece of furniture is more serious and should be filled in.

To fill in a scratch, use either a nutmeat (such as the meat of a walnut), a crayon in a color close to the shade of the furniture finish, a wax touch-up stick from a hardware, furniture, paint, or home center store, or shoe polish (the wax type) in a color close to the original finish.

Prevention is always better than cure. Use pads under hot dishes, coasters for glasses, and always supply plenty of ashtrays.

CHECKLIST FOR BUYING WOOD FURNITURE

Piece or Part	Check First	Plus Features	Valuable Extras
Back	Same wood as front	Finished same as front	Screwed in place
Drawers	Should not wobble or stick	Side or center glides	Dust panels
Joints	Type — refer to text	Adhesive together with screws	Corner blocks, hidden screws
Doors (hinged)	Tend to swing shut	Strong hinges	Magnetic catches
(sliding)	Grooves cut into wood		
Hardware	Solid	Firmly attached	Attractive
Tables	No sway when leaned on	Corner blocks at legs	Drop leaves firmly supported
Chairs	No sway	Corner blocks at legs	Legs even
Glass	Clear, flawless		
Legs	Even	Self-leveling casters	
Finish	Bottom, insides of drawers, etc., smooth, no checking or crazing	Evenly stained	

CARE, FEEDING, AND REPAIR OF WOOD FURNITURE

Furniture Finish	Regular Care	Polishing
Paint, synthetic lacquer, plastic finishes	Dust, wash with soap suds, dry thoroughly	Not needed; if desired, use only polish safe for painted surfaces
Glossy, non-synthetic (pre-1960)	Dust, buff	Polish or wax every six months; apply thin coat, buff thoroughly; avoid wax with silicones
Oil or natural finishes	Dust, buff	Polish or wax no more than four times a year; if necessary, wash with mild soap suds, dry thoroughly, then apply polish, oil, or wax

EMERGENCY CARE
USE ONLY IF BUFFING AND REPOLISHING FAILS

Problem	Cure
Alcohol (also perfume, some drugs), burns	Try masking with touch-up stick; if that fails, mix rottenstone and linseed oil (from a paint or hardware store); rub with the grain, polish
Candle wax	Crumble with finger, scrape with plastic spatula, polish
Heat marks (usually white)	Rub with furniture polish
Bloom (from humidity)	Add one tablespoon vinegar to one quart water on sponge and wring out; rub; follow by buffing and polishing
Water marks	Try masking with touch-up stick; ironing a blotter over mark may work
Scratches	Fill in with nutmeat, crayon, touch-up stick, or shoe polish

7

Buying Today's New Furniture

One of the most important trends which has developed during this century is that toward honest materials. Aspects of this trend range from a refusal even to look at anything other than such natural products as wood, cotton, straw, and so forth, to an appreciation of an honest use of the materials, including the synthetics that are available today. This means, for example, not trying to make plastic look like wood, but allowing it to look like plastic and taking advantage of its characteristics.

As a result of this movement, various types of furniture which do not fit into the traditional classifications have been developed. This chapter discusses some of the materials used for this furniture, offers buying advice, and suggests methods of care.

PLASTIC

We started this section by mentioning plastic furniture. It is probably the most significant type of furniture made today. The word *plastic*, in its general descriptive sense, refers to something that can be formed and shaped fairly easily. In the case of furniture, the word refers to the plastics from which chairs and tables can be molded into the desired shape, thereby eliminating certain important aspects of wood furniture making such as joints, finishing, and so forth.

Plastic furniture can be opaque or clear, giving the look of glass without the weight and risk of breakage of glass, or fabriclike. The clear plastics are usually acrylic plastic. Polystyrene and polyester, both of which can be made in bright colors or black and white, are two synthetics used in making the opaque plastics. Vinyl is often thought of as a fabric (it's used for raincoats, for instance), but it is also a plastic. Vinyl furniture usually consists of long tubes filled with air, water, or gelatin, as in a water bed, or chips, as in a bean bag chair. Vinyl plastic can be clear or opaque.

JUDGING PLASTIC FURNITURE

How do you judge plastic furniture?

To judge plastic furniture, taste — your taste — is extremely important. If you are unsure of your own taste but feel you want something in plastic to help create a certain mood in your home, take the time to study the different types of plastic furniture available. Look at store displays and, if there is a museum devoted to modern design near you, visit it. A good book on modern design can also help you educate your eye so you can develop your taste. Once you are fairly sure of your taste in this furniture you are ready to judge the quality of the furniture itself.

Start with the weight. Although plastic has the virtue of being lightweight, too light a weight probably indicates too thin a plastic. This is where shopping around and looking at different manufacturers' plastic furniture becomes important — you can't judge weight in a plastic until you have some basis of comparison. In addition to the fact that plastics which are too thin won't hold up under weight (they'll bend and sag), they can also break — and leave sharp spikes.

Since plastics are molded, look for smooth edges and surfaces. There should be no bubbles and the color should be even throughout the piece unless, of course, the color is swirled or shaded by intent for design. If the plastic furniture is of high quality, it will be smooth and finished on all sides.

Although plastics can be molded, some of the plastics, notably the clear acrylics, have more rigidity. These may be cut and joined. Check for smoothness of the joins.

Special Uses and Designs

Some plastic furniture combines plastic with upholstery. Polyurethane foam, for instance, may be covered with polyester fiberfill. The frame of such furniture may also be plastic — polyester, perhaps, reinforced with glass fiber.

Plastic is often colored and molded to resemble wood and then shaped into lightweight clocks, end tables, and parts for furniture which is made for the most part of wood. In this way, elaborate carving can be imitated. This use of plastic is frowned upon by most purists.

Plastic is also made into furniture which is considered more honest. Pedestal tables (only one leg, in the center) are an example of the best in plastic furniture design. Bright colored cubes which fit together to form tables or entire storage walls are another example of what is considered good plastic design.

ADVANTAGES AND DISADVANTAGES

Plastic furniture has definite advantages. We've already mentioned the lightness of weight. A second advantage is the variety of colors available.

At one time, American manufacturers, especially those using plastics for housewares, tended to use rather dull colors. Today, however, probably as a result of the European and Asian use of vivid colors for plastics, there is now much more variety.

Because plastics can be bent, furniture can be easily molded to the body. This is sometimes called "contouring." Solid wood furniture must be either carved to the body or padded (as in the case of upholstered furniture) to fit the body.

There are also disadvantages to plastic furniture.

Plastics — especially the acrylics — tend to get scratched and grow cloudy with time. Water beds have been known to leak; the filling has been known to come out of bean bag chairs. Some plastics break or bend when hit by hard blows or sharp objects or become distorted by heat. High-impact polystyrene is a plastic made to resist hard blows.

One of the virtues of plastic furniture is that it can be produced in quantity from one mold, eliminating the many non-automated steps which are necessary for most other types of furniture. In theory, this should lower the price. At present, however, high-quality plastic furniture is at least as expensive as any other good furniture.

CARE OF PLASTIC FURNITURE

Since plastic furniture cannot be harmed by water as wood can, you may choose to wash your plastic furniture rather than dust it. You may find that this is the only way you can get it really clean. Plastic furniture is often somewhat electrostatic, which means it may attact and hold dust. Use a damp sponge with soap suds or a dishwashing detergent. Never use a cleanser — it will scratch the plastic.

Plastics (especially the acrylics) get scratched very easily. This gives them a dull appearance after a time. Paste wax or a product especially made for plastic furniture, applied every four weeks or so to the tops of furniture and every six months to the legs and sides, helps protect plastic furniture from scratches and helps hide scratches which already exist. Eventually, however, the scratches may become serious enough to require resanding of the surface by a professional.

METAL AND GLASS

Metal and glass have recently become more popular as materials for home-use furniture.

Glass shelves are supported by highly polished chromium frames to form such pieces as coffee tables and étagères. This metal and glass combination has become a leading contemporary style. It has a quality of sophistication and lightness, but the lightness is deceptive — although the glass appears light it is extremely heavy.

These glass and chromium pieces become finger marked and dusty quickly. If you buy one of these tables, you will probably find you have to clean it every day. Use mild soap and water or a window-cleaning product.

In choosing glass and metal furniture, look for the same signs of quality you would look for in plastic furniture. The glass should be thick and well secured in the metal frame. The glass should be clear and absolutely flawless. The frame should be sturdy, well joined without rough edges, and smooth.

METAL

Several types of metal furniture have become popular for the home, including some which were previously limited to outdoor use. This outdoor or garden furniture — now occasionally called leisure furniture — has grown increasingly attractive. If you think you might ever use this furniture outside, be sure it is rustproof.

• *Aluminum* — which is light, non-rusting, and weather resistant — is perhaps the best metal for this type of furniture.

• *Wrought iron* is a popular metal for furniture used outside, for certain modern pieces ranging from bookcases to the butterfly chair, and for very elaborate adaptations of French designs on tables, chairs, and bed headboards. Wrought iron used outside will eventually rust if not protected sufficiently by paint. There are synthetic paints available that combine color with a rust inhibitor which can help prevent rusting. Paint wrought iron which is used outdoors all year every spring. If it is brought into the house during the winter, paint it as needed.

When shopping for wrought iron, look for a smooth finish, including the joints. Wrought iron tends to be somewhat rough, however, so don't look for a finish as smooth as you would find on, say, chromium.

The best care for wrought iron furniture is dusting. The easiest way to dust may be with the dusting attachment of a tank-type vacuum cleaner. Waxing improves the appearance of wrought iron but is not necessary. If you decide to wax, use a clear paste wax.

• *Chromium tubing* is popular for very casual metal furniture — folding outdoor chairs, for instance — and for some inexpensive indoor furniture items. This furniture is lightweight and practical but, as yet, lacks any design character. The tubing should be cared for by dusting and, when necessary, washing with immediate drying.

• A limited amount of *brass, copper, and silver* are used in furniture. These metals have many of the same characteristics as the chromium used in glass and metal furniture, so look for similar quality points. Brass, copper, and silver all tarnish. Use polishes specifically designed for each metal — a polish suitable for brass, for instance, is much too strong for silver and will actually wear some of the silver away.

• *Stainless steel*, also used in some metal furniture, does not tarnish. It benefits from washing in the same way chromium does.

WICKER

Wicker is another type of furniture traditionally associated with outdoor living which is moving indoors. Wicker is lightweight and, because of its open design, appears airy. It is made from small shoots of certain trees (willow, for instance) which are pliable enough to be interwoven. It is usually either finished with a protective coating which preserves its natural wood color or painted.

Wicker is best cleaned by dusting, most easily by the dusting attachment on a tank-type vacuum cleaner. Painted wicker may require periodic washing using soap suds, not detergent, on a sponge; rinse with clear water and dry immediately. Wicker is, however, difficult to wash because of its many surfaces. Avoid getting it more than damp in washing.

BUTCHER BLOCK

Butcher block furniture, usually made from a combination of strong woods joined in rectangles for additional strength, is an example of wood furniture that is "new" enough to belong in this chapter.

Butcher blocks, used by butchers for cutting up meat, are

sturdy, handsome, and clean lined. The surface has an elegance from the pattern created by the joining of the wood. Originally used only in kitchens, butcher blocks are now used in living rooms and elsewhere as handsome tables. Butcher block furniture usually has an oil finish and should be cared for like other oil-finished furniture.

PAPIER MACHÉ

Papier maché furniture, made from paper pulp mixed with an adhesive and hardened, was used for furniture in Victorian times. Today, there is little papier maché furniture being made but it is used for certain relatively small, decorative pieces.

Papier maché should be dusted rather than washed, as water may cause it to disintegrate.

CHECKLIST FOR BUYING TODAY'S NEW FURNITURE

Material	Basic Features	Features to Look For	Desirable Features
Plastic	Light but strong	Smooth edges and surfaces; even color (if any)	Comfort of contoured chairs
Metal and glass	Glass thick, frame sturdy	No rough edges; all surfaces smooth; flawless glass	
Wrought iron	Sturdy	Fairly smooth	Rust-inhibiting paint
Other metals	Suitable for use (e.g., aluminum for outdoors)	Smooth surfaces, well joined	
Wicker	Well finished	No rough ends	Comfort of chair; sturdiness of table
Butcher block	Same as other wood furniture (see chart, chapter 6, "Buying Wood Furniture")		

CARE OF TODAY'S NEW FURNITURE

Material	Cleaning Method
Plastic	Wash using damp sponge with soap suds or dishwashing detergent; never use abrasives, as plastic scratches; waxing may inhibit development of scratches; kits available to help remove scratches
Metal and glass	Wash with mild soap and water or window-cleaning product, polish immediately with paper towel
Metal	Dust with vacuum cleaner; wax adds protection but is not necessary; remove tarnish and polish brass, copper, and silver with polishes suitable for each
Wicker	Dust with vacuum cleaner; wash with soap suds, rinse with clear water, dry promptly
Butcher block	Care for same as natural oil finished furniture — see chart, chapter 6, ''Buying Wood Furniture''
Papier maché	Dust with dry cloth or vacuum cleaner only

8

Buying Upholstered Furniture

Upholstered furniture represents a fairly large financial investment. It takes up a lot of space, can last for years, and often determines whether a home appears — and is — comfortable or uncomfortable.

Upholstered furniture is furniture with a soft rather than hard seating area. Upholstered furniture may have springs or, in contemporary versions, depend for its comfort and upholstered effect on foam (usually either rubber or polyurethane). The springs or foam are then covered with cushions made of feathers, down, foam rubber, or one of the synthetics in foam or chip form. All is encased in fabric. This fabric is often referred to as the upholstery.

High-quality, expensive furniture is covered with muslin before the upholstery fabric is added. It is often sold "in the muslin" and can be either upholstered as desired or slip-covered.

The production of most upholstered furniture involves many steps. For this reason it is often possible to have a sofa or chair almost custom made. You may be able to have the back of a sofa, for instance, altered in shape to one you prefer to the floor sample. Such changes increase the price, but not as much as you may think. It's worth checking.

CHOOSING UPHOLSTERED FURNITURE

When you first shop for upholstered furniture, you may find the choice almost overwhelming. If, however, you keep in mind what you want, the choices narrow down.

Start with the size of furniture you want. Do you want a sofa? A chair? A love seat? Love seats are smaller than sofas, seating two people rather than the three or more most sofas seat.

Once you have decided on the piece of upholstered furniture you want, measure the space where it will go. Write down these measurements and take them with you when you shop. Sizes are extremely hard to carry in your head.

Sofas longer than six feet (72 inches) may pose special problems. Be sure the doors or windows of your home are large enough for the sofa to go through. If you live in an apartment, find out what is the largest size that can be brought through the building. The size of the elevator, if any, often determines this. Bringing furniture up the outside of the building and through a window, although possible in most places (and often necessary, as in the case of grand pianos), is expensive.

After you know the size you want think about the style. There is not as much styling choice in upholstered furniture as in other furniture. This is partly because upholstery is a relatively late development in the history of furniture. Mass producers of furniture tend to limit their styling to upholstered furniture items that will suit what they consider the broad range of American taste.

If you want a fairly authentic reproduction of, say, a Chippendale sofa, you will have to go to the more expensive manufacturers or even to custom furniture makers to find it. This kind of furniture is rarely fully displayed in a department or furniture store. Ask if there are catalogues you can look at to find the furniture you want. The reason few stores have very expensive furniture on display is that the sale is slow and the cost of the inventory is high.

If you are willing to buy a perfectly good but not outstanding piece of upholstered furniture, you will have little difficulty in finding it.

If you are buying a sofa or love seat, consider whether a sleep sofa might suit your space needs. Sleep sofas are discussed in depth in the section on bedding.

ALLERGIES

Consider the rest of your family in buying upholstered furniture from the point of view of allergies as well as taste. If anyone in the family is severely or even slightly allergic (hay fever, hives) it's wise to avoid kapok, hair, feathers, and wool even if that person has never shown an allergic reaction to any of these substances.

The reason for avoiding them is that allergies often develop as a result of repeated exposure to a particular substance. By avoiding the materials above, all of which are found in furniture and known to be common causes of allergies, you limit the number of exposures the allergic person will have.

If there is someone in your family with a very severe allergy, of course, you will probably find your decorating plans already defined and limited by the doctor.

How do you find out what upholstered furniture contains? Look for a tag — usually attached under the furniture or to one of the cushions — listing all the materials from which the furniture is made. Check it carefully.

Much upholstered furniture today is made of synthetic and rubber foam. Foam is considered to be almost allergy free, so that an allergy does not pose as serious a difficulty as it once did.

TRYING FURNITURE

Once you know what you want in upholstered furniture and have narrowed your choices down to certain pieces, try them out. It is essential to do this. You and your family will be sitting on that piece of furniture for a very long time.

Trying it out means sitting long enough to find out if it becomes noticeably less comfortable after a period of time. Trying is easier to say than to do. Furniture salespeople tend to become rather annoyed at people who sit on the furniture instead of buying it. Be firm.

Reclining Chair

If you are shopping for a reclining chair (also called an action chair) it is essential to try it out. These chairs are designed to fit your body, so be sure the chair you buy is right for your body.

Start by sitting in the chair and angling it to make sure it remains comfortable in all positions. If you plan to sit in a reclining chair to read or watch television, be sure you can do so in comfort.

The mechanism which makes a reclining chair recline is extremely important. Test it to be sure it moves smoothly and easily. It is worth shopping around for a recliner which has a warranty on this operating mechanism.

Not all recliners merely recline. Some other action features include swiveling and rocking. Choose the chair for comfort and ease of operation. If a comfortable recliner with a good mechanism also has other features, take advantage of them if you like them.

QUALITY INDICATIONS IN UPHOLSTERED FURNITURE

Certain points should be checked for quality before you buy any piece of upholstered furniture.

It's not a bad idea to bounce up and down on the upholstered furniture to start. In this way you can discover whether the springs are likely to creak and whether they are good enough to keep you from hitting the frame. Bouncing will also tell you if the frame is sturdy or if it has a tendency to wobble. If the furniture salesperson tells you not to bounce because it will break the furniture, you'll know it isn't up to top standards.

Here are specific points to check.

• *Frame*. Most upholstered furniture frames are wood and many of the features that determine quality in wood furniture are the same for the frames of upholstered furniture. For instance, the frame should have corner blocks which are screwed, glued, and perhaps reinforced. These are designed to support the corners and keep them from wobbling.

• The *legs* of the best furniture are made in one piece with the back. If they are separate and screwed on to the back, they should be joined by one of the better construction methods discussed in the section on wood furniture.

• *Springs*. Traditional upholstered furniture has springs. (Much modern or contemporary furniture is made from molded plastic of one kind or another and omits springs.) Coil springs are spiral shaped, made of metal. Sinuous springs, also metal, are flat and wavy.

The purpose of springs is to give furniture the "bounce" we mentioned earlier. They are also used to obtain a desired shape. Both types of springs may be used in the same piece of furniture in different places. Coil springs are usually used to support the frame of the furniture.

Speaking generally, the more springs the better.

• The term *hand-tied* with reference to coil springs describes how the springs are joined to each other. This tying is done with string. The more ties the better. An eight-way tie is considered best; four-way is satisfactory.

• The bottom of the spring area of upholstered furniture is reinforced. In high-quality furniture, this reinforcement is bands of steel covered by fabric, often burlap. In addition, webbing (woven bands of fabric) covers the springs. On high-quality furniture the webbing traditionally has been jute. Jute, however, is an imported fabric and manufacturers have recently been using domestic synthetic fibers such as polypropylene (olefin) for their webbing.

The bands of webbing must be close together to do any good. If you can put your fist between the bands easily, they are too far apart.

• *Sinuous springs* have become more popular as upholstered furniture has become slimmer. They may be used with fabric-covered coil springs or alone. They are usually found only in the back of upholstered furniture.

• *Padding* is what gives upholstered furniture its upholstered nature. The padding is usually a fluffy layer of fabric such as reprocessed wool — the type used for interlining a winter coat. The best furniture has two or three layers of padding covering the frame. This makes the furniture softer and more comfortable. Often, layers of thinner fabric are placed between the layers of padding.

• *Cushions* on upholstered furniture are usually separate

from the main part of the furniture. They can be made in various ways. The type you select (or settle for) is up to you; they can all meet quality standards. Take into account comfort, allergies, and price.

Expensive furniture is often made with spring-down cushions. For this construction, coil springs are covered with muslin, then placed into fabric with a slab of some synthetic such as polyurethane. Down is then blown into a covering which is wrapped around the spring-filled center.

All-down or all-feather cushions are relatively rare today in new furniture but you may find them on imported, antique, or hand-me-down furniture. These are considered the softest of cushions, but are the kind that require plumping up after use.

In recent years, foam — polyurethane or rubber — has come to almost dominate the cushion market in upholstered furniture. Foam is not as soft as the spring-down, all-down, or feather construction and many people prefer it for its firmness. These cushions do not have to be plumped up.

Polyurethane foam may be called *polyfoam* by salespeople. This type of cushion usually starts as a slab and may be covered with polyester in chip or fiberfill form before being covered by the upholstery.

Latex foam cushions are another form of synthetic cushion. They are more expensive than polyurethane. Foam rubber as a cushion material is extremely comfortable but after a time the foam rubber changes into a sawdustlike material. There are claims that this problem has been (or is being) overcome.

FLAMMABILITY

The very thing which makes certain upholstery soft — the fact that air can surround the material from which it is made — also means that once a fire starts it tends to smolder and, because of the oxygen from the air, is difficult to put out. Recently, laws have been passed or are under discussion regarding the flammability of upholstered furniture. Furniture for such places as motels, for instance, must meet certain flammability standards for safety. This is because upholstery fires tend to be extremely serious. To lessen the flammability of furniture, there will be furniture made with different features from those mentioned above within the next decade.

MAKING COMPROMISES

In this section of the book we have told you what are generally considered the best qualities for upholstered furniture to have. It is very possible that when you shop for such furniture you will not be able to find these characteristics at all or will be able to find them only in a style or at a price which you do not want.

You will find yourself making compromises. For instance, the ideal is that the legs of furniture should be made in one with the back. Because it is so easy for such legs to be broken off in delivery, you may have to buy furniture with screw-on legs. The legs are unscrewed for delivery and when the furniture arrives you (or, if you're lucky, an obliging delivery man) will screw the legs on.

Our discussion of interior construction features provides another example. You will find there is a great deal of furniture today made with no springs at all. It may be made from molded plastic covered with padding and then with fabric or from foam (polyurethane or rubber) which is then padded and upholstered. You will have to make your own decision on these compromises, but these pieces of furniture often last as long if not longer than the traditionally made pieces. See the discussions of furniture delivery and fabric for information on these subjects. Care of upholstered furniture is covered in chapter 11, "Fabrics for Home Furnishings."

CHECKLIST FOR BUYING TRADITIONALLY MADE UPHOLSTERED FURNITURE

Feature	Test
Comfort	Sit for a period of time to determine whether back, sides, and seat fit and are comfortable; bounce to test springs and sturdiness; springs should not creak
Frame	Check as for wood furniture, look for corner blocks; legs made in one piece with back
Springs	Furniture with more springs is more satisfactory; eight-way tie of coil springs is best; four-way tie is satisfactory
Reinforcement	Best reinforcement of springs is steel bands covered by burlap; webbing should be close enough together so fist cannot go through
Padding	Furniture should have two or three layers of padding over frame
Cushions	Comfortable; well-covered

CHECKLIST FOR BUYING NONTRADITIONALLY MADE UPHOLSTERED FURNITURE

Feature	Test
Comfort	Sit for a period of time to determine whether back, sides, and seat fit and are comfortable; bounce to test sturdiness
Frame	Squeeze frame with fingers; should not give excessively unless this is a design feature
Cushions	Should be comfortable
Plastic parts	Should be solid and sturdy, unscratched

9

Buying Bedding

Most of us will spend one-third of our lives in bed, so the bedding we choose should be right for us and right for sleeping. On the other hand, although bedding is important, some advice about it has overemphasized its role in our lives to the point where some of us find shopping for bedding the most difficult furniture shopping we do.

In this chapter, we will once again discuss both the ideal and the possible so that you will be sufficiently informed to make your own decisions wisely.

WHEN TO BUY

When should you replace the bedding you already own? Here are some ways to know if you need new bedding.

• A lumpy, bumpy mattress is not a good one; a squeaking mattress indicates that the mattress is not supporting you properly.

• If, when you are sleeping in another bed, you find the mattress a good deal more comfortable than the one you have at home, you need a new mattress.

• Finally, don't concentrate only on your own bedding and

ignore other beds in your home. Good hosts and hostesses
sleep on guest room beds at least once a year as a test.

HOW TO SHOP

Shopping for a mattress is somewhat more complicated
than it was once because there are now foam mattresses as
well as innerspring mattresses. There are things common to
both types to consider in choosing a mattress, and we'll discuss
these points first.

FIRMNESS

Firmness is an important consideration. Unfortunately,
although mattresses are labeled with descriptive terms such
as "medium firm," "regular firm," "super firm," and "extra
firm," there is no standard definition of these terms. In fact,
"firmness" has become so desirable that the label "soft" seems
to have disappeared.

This lack of standardization means you have to try out the
mattress in the store. You have to make your own judgement.
Although the advice about trying out a mattress in a store is
time-honored, it is difficult to lie down in the middle of the day
in the middle of your local store's bedding department. The
most you can hope is that you will get some impression of
which mattress feels most comfortable to you.

The mattress should support your body, keep your spine
straight, and feel right. There should be neither too much
bounce nor too little. A good deal has been said about the
importance of avoiding a too soft mattress. You can also run
into trouble with a too firm mattress.

The too soft mattress won't support your back properly; it
may give you a backache that goes away after you've been out
of bed for a time. The too hard mattress may give you a stiff
neck or make your fingers and toes go numb. If you must
choose between a too soft and a too firm mattress, however,
the too firm one seems best. The Japanese, for instance, have
managed without soft mattresses for years. The firmness
should not be so stiff, however, that you feel you are about to
roll off the bed.

If you are planning to share a double bed (called full-size by the furniture industry) but you and your partner can't agree on a mattress, forget the idea of sharing. Instead, settle for two twin-size mattresses and use them over one large box spring. Box springs are discussed later in this chapter.

BED SIZES

The size and type of the bed for which you are buying a mattress will also affect the mattress you buy. For instance, if you are buying a mattress for a very narrow bed, such as that usually called "cot size," you may not be able to find anything but a very firm foam mattress.

The sizes of mattress are not standard, any more than the meaning of the word *firm* is. There is, however, an easy rule for deciding what length of mattress you need. The mattress should be at least six inches longer than the tallest sleeper. Here is a rough guide to mattress sizes.

• *Youth, cot, rollaway folding bed,* and *divan* mattresses are usually between 27″ wide and 48″ wide and between 72″ and 75″ long.

• *Twin-size* mattresses are 38″ to 39″ wide and 75″ long. The *extra-long twin* size is 80″.

• The *standard double* (often called *full-size*) mattress is 53″ or 54″ wide by 75″, the *extra-long double* 53″ or 54″ wide and 80″ long.

• The *queen-size* mattress is usually 60″ wide by 80″ long and the *king-size* mattress 76″ by 80″.

Much has been made in recent years of the fact that the average baby's crib mattress is 27″ or 28½″ wide and that this is about the same space the standard double bed gives each sleeper. This is a fascinating statistic but not really important. A baby spends many of his waking hours in his crib and his sleeping hours are much longer than ours. If you feel crowded in a double bed you may want one of the larger sizes. If not, there is no reason to feel you must have a larger mattress.

Keep in mind that if you buy queen-size or king-size mattresses you will pay significantly more for all the other elements of your bedding (sheets, blankets, bedspreads) over the years.

Many mattresses come with some kind of guarantee. Be sure you know exactly what it covers and be sure you have it in writing.

FLAMMABILITY

Flammability standards, to protect people from fire, are in effect for all mattresses manufactured after December 1973. It is unlikely that mattresses made before this date are still on the market. The reason for the standards is that mattress fires tend to smolder for a long time, are hard to extinguish, and are often fatal. Even with the new flammability standards, smoking in bed is a poor idea. There is just too much risk of fire.

INNERSPRING MATTRESSES

Innerspring mattresses are probably the best-known mattress type and certainly the best promoted and advertised. These mattresses are made in layers with insulating material and padding on each side of a unit which contains coils. These coils are the springs.

When the coils in one section of the mattress are pushed down, as when someone lies on one side of the bed, other coils near that section should not be affected.

Advertising often emphasizes the number of coils in an innerspring mattress. Actually, this figure is relatively unimportant. Some mattresses may have large coils — say, 200 to 300 — tied together. Other mattresses have hundreds of small coils in fabric pockets. The two types of coils are not really comparable. The small ones are made of a lighter gauge of wire than the larger, and both types of mattress can be excellent.

Most experts agree that at least 250 coils are needed for a good mattress. With more than 300 coils there is no change; you are safe in choosing a mattress solely on the basis of comfort.

A coating on the coils so they won't be noisy and special insulating materials to keep you from feeling the coils are advantages.

All mattresses should have at least four small places for

ventilation. These usually have metal or plastic perforated circles over them.

As in buying upholstered furniture, check the label giving mattress contents. If anyone who will sleep on it is allergic, buy a foam mattress.

Innerspring mattresses should be turned regularly. Turn a mattress by flopping it so the head is at the foot and what was the top becomes the bottom. This distributes the wear and keeps the mattress from wearing out in one place too quickly. Most experts recommend turning the mattresses once a week, when the beds are changed. It's a big job. Two people make it easier. Innerspring mattresses should have well-secured handles to help in turning.

Ticking (mattress covering) is discussed in the chapter on fabrics for home decorating.

FOAM MATTRESSES

Two kinds of foam are used in mattresses — polyurethane foam and latex foam. Polyurethane, a synthetic, is a fairly recent arrival on the market, so it may develop some durability problems which are not yet known. So far, it seems to hold up well, and although the foam itself yellows when exposed to air this does not seem to affect its performance. Latex foam rubber, however, has had the disadvantage of eventually turning into a sawdustlike material as a result of crystallization. Manufacturers claim that this problem is solved or about to be solved.

Both types of foam have similar advantages: quietness (there are no springs to be noisy); lack of allergy-producing materials; and a smoothness innerspring mattresses can't have. They are also free from such enemies of innerspring mattresses as mildew and moths.

One of the biggest advantages of foam mattresses is that they are very lightweight compared with innerspring mattresses. Changing sheets is much easier.

Foam mattresses do not need to be turned. They do not become crushed from weight as innerspring mattresses do.

Foam mattresses are usually less expensive than innerspring mattresses and many people find them more comfortable. These people feel that even the firmest of innerspring mattresses have too much bounce and too many uneven places, due to their construction.

Latex foam rubber is either made by the pincore method (lots of tiny holes) or honeycomb method (large holes). Polyurethane foam is made in slabs which are cut to size. Polyurethane foam is the least expensive mattress material.

Foam mattresses are usually about 4″ to 6″ thick. The thickness is relatively unimportant. Don't pay more than you need for a foam mattress. Some manufacturers are adding "improvements" to foam — padding and so forth — to make these mattresses look more like innerspring mattresses. These additions raise the price and do not improve performance.

You may have difficulty finding an "unimproved" foam mattress in a conventional department or furniture store. These stores, understandably anxious to make money, tend to offer foam only with the extras. Check unfinished furniture stores for a basic foam mattress. They often offer such mattresses to fit the beds they make which come in all the popular sizes.

Ticking for foam mattresses, as for innerspring mattresses, is discussed in the section on home furnishing fabrics.

BOX SPRINGS

It is usually believed that box springs are essential for proper support and comfort in bed and that they should be used with a mattress of any type. Actually, they add to the comfort of an innerspring mattress, but are unimportant with a foam mattress.

The purpose of a box spring is to add an extra to the work the mattress does. The springs cushion your weight as you move in bed. Never use a worn-out box spring — it's better not to have one at all.

Box springs consist of springs (coils of wire) fitted into a boxlike frame. The springs are similar to those used in innerspring mattresses but are larger and the wire is heavier. The springs are supported either by a metal frame or wooden slats, are tied together, and are covered with a layer of padding (usually cotton, felt, or horsehair) and then with ticking that matches the mattress.

The only reason for having a matching box spring and mattress is to be sure they are made for each other. Then, too, bedding is often sold as a set. You may be able to save money by buying the box spring and mattress at the same time. There are frequent sales on bedding; check one of these before buying bedding at the usual price.

Foam mattresses do not need box springs. The foam mattress gives a different type of support from an innerspring mattress, and this type of support does not require additional springs underneath.

Many people, however, prefer to use a box spring with a foam mattress, either because of tradition or to raise the sleeping surface of the bed to the height it would have with traditional bedding. To do this, you will need an extra-deep box spring. Foam mattresses are not as deep as innerspring mattresses.

For the allergic person, of course, these box springs are out of the question. There is no point in buying a nonallergenic mattress and then putting it on a potentially allergenic box spring.

A relatively new development in bedding is the foam box spring. These are sold for use with foam mattresses, often as a set. They simply make the mattress higher, often raising it to the height the average bed requires. Since these box springs are made exactly like the foam mattresses, they do not have the same quality indications as with true box springs.

Foam mattresses do very well without a box spring, and many beds, such as some double-decker beds and some of the modern slab or platform wood beds, are designed to be used without box springs. Innerspring mattresses can also be used this way, but many people miss the extra bounce of the box spring.

CARE OF MATTRESSES AND BOX SPRINGS

The care of mattresses and box springs is fairly simple. It helps to vacuum them regularly, perhaps once a month. Innerspring mattresses should be turned regularly.

BED FOR SITTING AND SLEEPING

Bed pads, which protect the mattress from perspiration and provide a more comfortable sleeping surface, should be used under the bottom sheet. Mattress covers, which encase the mattress completely, protect it from dust and a certain amount of staining and are used by some fastidious people. However, a mattress pad should be used in addition to a mattress cover.

Children's beds should have a rubber sheet under the pad (not on top — it makes a bed too hot) as long as necessary. Nowadays this "rubber sheet" will probably not be rubber but one of the synthetics which is impervious to liquids.

SLEEPING-SITTING FURNITURE

With houses growing smaller and people anxious to get their money's worth from every room, items that serve more than one purpose have become increasingly important in furnishing a home. This includes furniture that by day is a sofa or chair and by night a bed.

The simplest combination sleeping-sitting item is a twin-

or cot-size bed, covered with a spread that looks more living room than bedroom, with bolsters along the back. This is popular for the rooms of older children and in first apartments.

Twin-size beds may need additional cushions to be comfortable as a sitting place. In addition to bolsters (wedge-shaped or rectangular cushions) against the wall, pillows, including the bed pillow, covered to match the bedspread, can be used to make the seating area more comfortable.

Bed frames are sold in the same department in most stores as mattresses and box springs. Bed frames are metal frames designed to support a box spring and mattress. They are usually on casters which can be locked so that the bed will not roll unless required. They can be used either on their own or with some of the headboards that are sold separately.

Some chairs and ottomans, or large hassocks, turn into single beds. The ottomans usually open up, the chairbeds usually have a back which drops down. These are usually narrow (about 27″) but are normal bed length.

A studio couch is a sofa which turns into a bed when the back drops down so that it is even with the seat. This then provides a sleeping surface.

Another versatile sleeping arrangement is the so-called riser bed. This consists of two mattresses; one placed over the other when the bed is used as a single bed. It can open to be used as a double bed or to form two twin beds.

SOFA BEDS

The sofa bed is the item most people think of when they think of dual-purpose furniture. Sofa beds are also called sleep sofas and convertible sofas.

The cushions (which provide additional comfort when sofa beds are used as sofas) are usually removed. The seat section then unfolds. There is a double bed inside (the width depends on the width of the sofa) with a one-piece mattress.

At one time, these sofas were bulky and high and obviously sofa beds. Today, there are sleek versions, including some imported ones, and sleep sofas rarely look as if they're going to turn into a bed.

SOFA BED

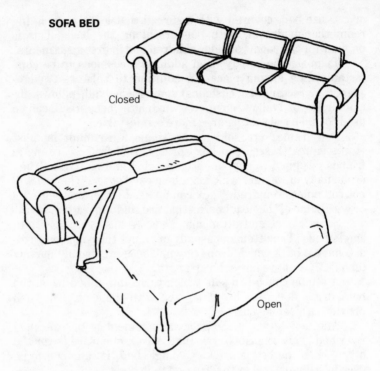

Closed

Open

SHOPPING FOR SLEEPING-SITTING FURNITURE

In buying a sofa bed or any other dual-purpose piece of furniture, you'll discover that often what makes a good bed does not make a good sofa, and vice versa. You may have to make compromises, either in terms of the styling of the sofa or in terms of the bed.

If a sofa bed is to be used every day for both sitting and sleeping — and many are — give it the tests listed for both upholstered furniture and for mattresses.

Some sofa beds come with a choice of mattress type, so read that section in this chapter before making a decision.

Most important, make sure that you — not the salesperson — find it easy to open and close the sofa bed. The frame should be sturdy and the legs which support the foot of the bed section should be strong, not spindly.

In many sleep sofas mattress sizes are different from the standard mattress sizes. The length is usually no longer than 75" because the bed needs to fold into a relatively small space.

Many sofa beds are much heavier than the average sofa. See if you can lift the sofa bed before buying it. If you can't, be sure it has casters so you can move it to clean under it or have casters added. Some sofa beds can be tilted forward so you can clean underneath.

See chapter 11, "Fabrics for Home Furnishings," for information on choosing upholstery for a sofa bed.

CHECKLIST FOR BUYING INNERSPRING MATTRESSES

Feature	Test
Comfort	Sufficient support for body; keeps spine straight; bounce seems comfortable
Available in desired size	If not, forget this mattress or buy a new bed
Coils	Move independently; at least 250; coating and insulation a plus
Ventilation	Four small holes in sides
Handles	Well-secured for turning mattress

CHECKLIST FOR BUYING BOX SPRINGS

Feature	Test
Springs	Supported by metal frame or wooden slats
Padding	Thick enough to protect springs from coming through ticking

CHECKLIST FOR BUYING FOAM MATTRESSES

Feature	Test
Comfort	Sufficient support for body; spine feels straight; bounce seems comfortable
Thickness	Thick enough (4″ to 6″) to support body
Size	Correct for bed

CHECKLIST FOR BUYING SOFA BEDS

Feature	Test
Appearance	Attractive as a sofa, not unnecessarily bulky
Comfort	As sofa, cushions body; as bed, supports body and keeps spine straight, comfortable
Opening	Easy for one person to open and close
Frame	Sturdy; not too wobbly as bed is opened and closed
Legs	All legs strong, including ones which support foot section of bed
Weight	Can be moved for cleaning, has casters, or tilts forward

10
Window Treatments

Windows are put into our houses to control light and air. They are usually made of glass or a synthetic plastic such as acrylic, or, in the tropics, of movable strips of metal or glass called louvers. Some windows are made of stained glass in whole or in part; the light filtering through this colored glass gives another look.

Because windows are designed to let in light, they create a problem in assuring privacy. How much privacy you want or require depends on how isolated your home may be, your attitude toward others seeing you, and, of course, whether you feel window coverings add to the appearance of your rooms.

The placement, size, and general look of the windows themselves can also affect the entire appearance of a room. This effect can be changed or enhanced by the window treatment.

This chapter includes a discussion of various types of window coverings, the different shapes of windows, and suggestions for decorating windows, including those which often create problems. A discussion of fabrics for curtains and draperies will be found in the chapter on fabrics for the home.

SHADES AND BLINDS

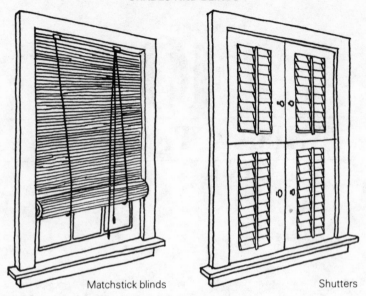

Matchstick blinds   Shutters

WINDOW COVERINGS

SHADES AND BLINDS

The words *shade* and *blind* are used interchangeably, though *shade* sometimes means one solid piece of window covering while *blind* (especially if it is a venetian blind) sometimes means a sectional window covering. Both are hung inside the window frame and flat against the window in most cases.

Shades and blinds are made so that they can completely cover the window. Some roller shades, also called roller blinds, cut out all light; others permit filtered light to enter a room.

Until fairly recently, shades and blinds were strictly functional in most American homes. The shades tended to be solid white or off-white, or sometimes green. Venetian blinds tended to have white slats only.

Today, roller shades can make a fashion statement by being covered with a fabric which coordinates with the up-

SHADES AND BLINDS

Roller shade with fabric cover

Venetian blinds

Roman shades

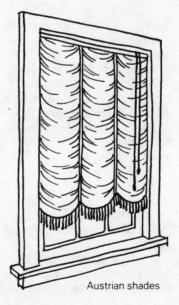

Austrian shades

holstery or drapery in a room. Fabric can be ironed onto the shade material easily. Kits containing rollers and fusible shade material are available.

Venetian blinds now come in a variety of colors and also with slats that run vertically rather than horizontally. Other types of shades include Roman and Austrian shades. Both these types are made of fabric shirred onto specially designed hardware. The shades are raised and lowered by strings at the side, as are venetian blinds, with the material being gathered more closely as the shades are raised. Austrian shades retain some shirring when down. Both instructions and the hardware necessary for making these shades are available at home centers and in drapery fabric departments and stores.

Other types of shades or blinds include those made of strips of wood. Matchstick blinds, for instance, are made of very narrow strips of wood. These blinds roll up on themselves; when they are lowered, they permit a minimum of light to filter between the pieces of wood.

SHUTTERS

Shutters are wooden doorlike objects which close over windows. For large windows, the shutters may be made in two sections so they can be folded back on themselves when they are open.

Shutters have long been used (in recent years, mainly for decoration) on the outside of houses. There has been a revival in their use inside houses since the early 1960s. Shutters for inside use are available in solid or louvered (slatted) form. In some slatted shutters the slats cannot actually be moved. Indoor shutters give a currently popular, informal look to a home.

CURTAINS

Curtains, like shades, blinds, and shutters, are set on the inside of the window frame. Curtains usually stop at the windowsill.

Curtains are often thought of as being made of sheer rather than opaque fabrics. Glass curtains are very sheer curtains designed to permit people to see out while blocking or

CURTAINS, DRAPERIES

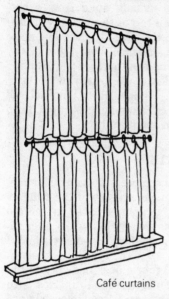

Café curtains

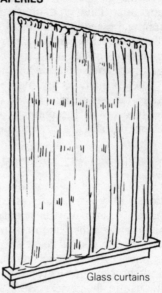

Glass curtains

Organdy tiebacks

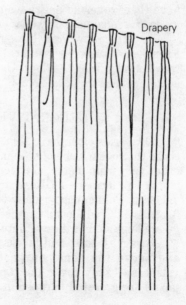

Drapery

limiting the view from outside because of the way light hits the curtains. This type of curtain is usually hung from a curtain rod placed on the inside of the top of the window frame. These curtains can fall straight to the sill of the window or be held back about one-third of the distance from the sill. Organdy tieback curtains are an example of this type of curtain.

Café curtains are hung in at least two tiers. One rod usually is placed inside the top of the window frame, another rod halfway down the window. Café curtains hang straight from their rods and are often made of an opaque fabric.

DRAPERIES

Draperies are more formal and more elaborate than curtains. They are usually hung from the outside of the window frame, often covering it entirely. Draperies can open on one side or the other or in the middle, usually be means of cords attached to special rods. Draperies can be pleated or gathered in many different ways depending upon the type of rod chosen and the type of pleater tape (stiff fabric designed specifically for use in draperies) used. A popular use for draperies is to have them cover an entire wall. Draperies are almost always made of an opaque, fairly heavy fabric.

In extremely formal rooms (those decorated with fine French furniture, for instance) draperies may be so long that they actually lie on the floor. Usually, however, they extend to about one inch from the floor.

DECORATIVE HEADINGS

Draperies often have some kind of decorative heading to cover the rods which hold them. These can be made of wood or other very rigid material, covered with paint or with fabric to match the draperies. These are called pelmets, cornices, or valances. Pelmets are usually two-dimensional and are placed flat above the windows. Cornices are usually made in a rectangular shape so that they jut into the room.

Swags, jabots, and fabric valances are made from fabric and serve the same purpose as pelmets, cornices, and valances — they cover the top of the rods. Both swags and jabots are gracefully draped in folds of fabric. A swag usually

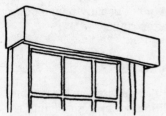

Cornice (Wood box, often covered)

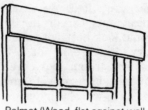

Pelmet (Wood, flat against wall
or window)

Fabric valance (Flat against wall or
window; may be
on rod. When not fabric,
same as pelmet)

Swag

Jabot

covers only the top of a window. A jabot usually hangs down over the side of the window and is often ruffled.

KINDS OF WINDOWS

To choose which of the many different window treatments you want, it is necessary, in addition to analyzing your requirements concerning privacy, to decide which treatment would look best with the decorative scheme of your home. A very formal room, for instance, almost demands draperies; an informal room looks well with tieback curtains, a fabric-covered shade, or café curtains. The kind and shape of window you have will also influence your choice.

DOUBLE-HUNG WINDOWS

Probably the best-known type of window is the double-hung window. This is the window which slides up and down in the frame. Double-hung windows in themselves usually present few problems in decorating. These are the windows for which most ready-made curtains are designed.

CASEMENT WINDOWS

Casement windows are windows which open like a door in the center or at the sides. They usually open outward. In decorating casement windows, allowance must be made to permit them to swing open and a way must be found to keep curtains or draperies from flapping.

FRENCH WINDOWS

French doors and French windows work very much like casement windows. They extend to the floor and can be used as doors. They usually open to the outside and again you will need to find a way to keep the window covering from flapping.

RANCH WINDOWS

Ranch windows are found in the so-called ranch houses built in the 1950s and 1960s. Ranch windows are placed very

WINDOWS

Double-hung window

Double-hung window

Casement window

French door or window

WINDOWS

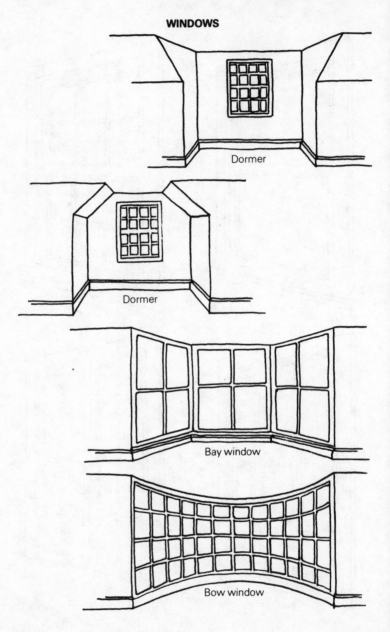

Dormer

Dormer

Bay window

Bow window

WINDOWS

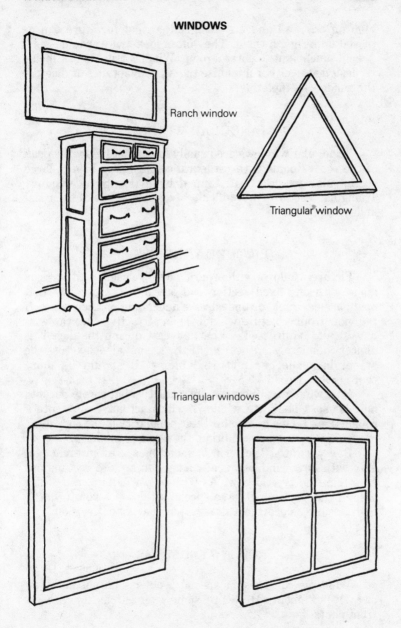

Ranch window

Triangular window

Triangular windows

high on the wall and are designed so that furniture can be placed underneath them. They often look awkward and don't permit much light to enter a room. Window treatments should be designed to either minimize their disadvantages or disguise the windows completely.

TRIANGULAR WINDOWS

Triangular windows are usually found just below the peak of the roof. Rooms with cathedral ceilings may have a large rectangular window wall topped by a triangular window. Triangular windows are difficult to dress because of their size and location.

PICTURE WINDOWS

Picture windows, either permanently closed in all parts or made with one fixed section and one or more sections that open, are desirable or undesirable depending on their view. If the view from a picture window is an attractive one, the window should be dressed so that, at least during the day, it is almost completely uncovered. If the window looks across the street into another picture window, it should be more thoroughly covered.

Bow windows are extremely attractive but rarely put into new houses. They are windows which actually curve into a rounded area. One reason for their popularity is the cozy quality they give a room; in addition, they let more light in.

Bay windows (the term is sometimes used interchangeably with bow windows) are windows in a more rectangular area than the typical bow. As with bow windows, the entire area of the bay should have special attention, even if you finally decide to decorate it the same as the rest of the room.

SOLVING PROBLEMS

Windows can present special problems because of their size or placement. Here are some suggestions for window treatments.

Ranch windows need either an inconspicuous covering or total disguise. For the inconspicuous treatment, a single curtain works well, preferably in a fabric which matches the walls. If you prefer total disguise for a ranch window, you will probably choose to cover the entire wall. Get a drapery rod which fits flush against the wall for this. If you cannot find one at your local hardware store, try to find a store which specializes in draperies.

If you have a bow window, and the bow is large enough, the area of the room surrounded by the bow should be treated separately from the rest of the room. It can be used as a reading corner, have a wide window seat added to it, hold a dining table or small round table, or the floor can be covered with a tray, pebbles, and plants.

For decorating the windows in the bow, the choice is actually one of mood, between, for instance, the informal, light-hearted mood of gingham or organdy tieback curtains and the greater formality of full-length draw draperies on a curved rod. If you choose to use tiebacks, you may find it is better to tie back the end curtains on each side of the bow and use only a valance of matching fabric above the middle windows.

Curved rods can be found in stores specializing in draperies and drapery hardware.

Bay windows often consist of a series of double-hung windows. The many straight lines in such a group of windows give a somewhat stiff effect. For this reason, bay windows often benefit from window coverings that stress curved lines. Any kind of looped fabric, from swags to a rounded valance to tiebacks, can help soften this look.

Picture windows have become so common recently that they have been receiving a great deal of imaginative decorating thought. If you want to cover a picture window, or if you have a window which is small or awkwardly placed so that it seems to cut up the wall, you may want to hang a drapery all the way across the wall.

For a less formal treatment, café curtains can be used on a picture window, with simple hanging side draperies or tiebacks. Because café curtains stress horizontal lines, they tend to cut the height of a room. The hanging side draperies are suggested to offset this effect.

You don't have to use curtains or draperies at all if you

WINDOW TREATMENTS

Picture window

Glass curtains with tiebacks

Drapery

don't want to. You can try sliding panels, for instance, perhaps made from Japanese shoji screens with translucent panels. These can either be fastened to the wall with hinges like shutters or placed in a track.

Triangular windows offer several different possible ways of decorating. The simplest is to leave the triangle alone and start the draperies where the sides of the window are parallel. If you want the triangle covered, you can get a rod which covers the top of the triangle; the curtains or draperies then drape at one side or the other. It may be difficult to find this ready made, but you can always draw a picture of the window when you take the measurements and arrange to have the rod custom made. You can also use an ordinary drapery rod, fixing it to the slanted side of the triangle. If the window peaks at the center, you will need two rods. This means the rod will be placed at a slant. With such a treatment, plan the draperies so that when they are closed the bottom edges will be even. This means that when the draperies are open there will be extra fabric on the floor, but this is a relatively minor consideration.

OTHER WINDOW PROBLEMS

There are other window problems which can be disguised by the window treatment.

One wall of a room may have two windows of wildly different types. Occasionally, for instance, a very short, high ranch window will be on the same wall as a large picture window. If the lack of balance between these two windows doesn't bother you, or only bothers you moderately, you can treat one of them inconspicuously (probably the ranch window) by covering it with a curtain or shade that is the same pattern or color as the walls. The other window on this wall can then be treated as if it were the only one.

If the lack of balance is very obvious, the best solution is to treat the two windows as one. This means, at its simplest, a wall of drapery fabric. Other possibilities include a wide shade covered to coordinate with the room and accented with draperies at the side of the wall.

Some windows are ugly through no fault of their own. For example, some have appeared to be the only place in a room to put the air conditioner and the radiator.

WINDOW TREATMENTS

Triangular windows

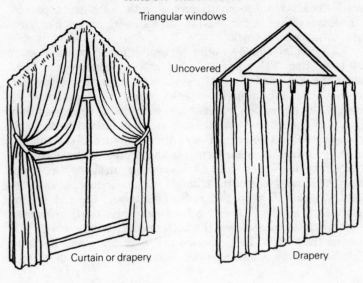

Uncovered

Curtain or drapery

Drapery

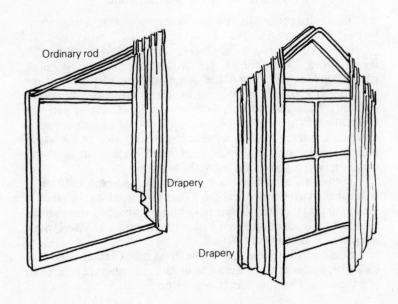

Ordinary rod

Drapery

Drapery

WINDOW TREATMENTS

Two different windows on one wall

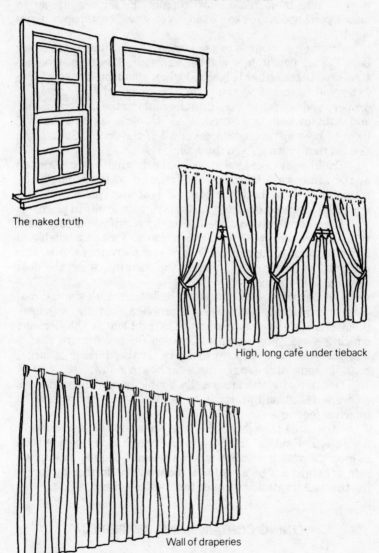

The naked truth

High, long café under tieback

Wall of draperies

Start by looking at the air conditioner. The finish on the air conditioner is not sacred, although most people act as if it were. There is no reason not to paint the air conditioner to match your walls. You can even cover it with wallpaper if you want.

Another solution is to use curtains and draperies to cover both the air conditioner and the radiator. These must be designed so that neither is blocked when you want to use it. Use extension brackets to bring the placement of the curtain or drapery rod out far enough into the room so the air conditioner and radiator will be covered. Your draperies or curtains will have to be wide enough to cover all of the rod, including the section that juts out from the wall.

Traditionally, casement and French windows are treated in the same way. Curtains are fastened to the windows by means of rods at both the top and bottom. This means that when the windows open the curtains remain firmly in place.

If you find this treatment somewhat stiff, you may want to look at a rod made for French doors. This is available at home centers, some hardware stores, and drapery shops. It is designed to swing away, holding the curtains, when the door or window is opened.

Dormer windows — windows built out from a slanted roof — are sometimes considered a problem, but the windows themselves aren't the problem. The problem is the dormer, which is usually too small to be used for much more than a window seat or a chest of drawers. If the dormer is large, consider some of the suggestions for bow windows.

Dormer windows are usually double-hung. Their curtains or draperies should probably be informal as dormers have an informal feeling.

Give some thought to the way you treat the slanting ceiling on either side of the dormer. Although many people tend to stop the wall treatment where the slant begins, an impression of height can be added to a room with a dormer by carrying the wall treatment up over the slanted ceiling.

·LINING CURTAINS AND DRAPERIES

Think about lining your curtains and draperies. Curtains and draperies, except sheer ones, benefit from lining. Lining makes them hang better and last longer, as it protects the inside from the effects of sunlight.

Don't think that the lining must be dull and uninteresting — consider how your windows will look from the outside. If, for instance, you have a solid green fabric for the draperies in the living room, think about using a green print lining.

Lining your draperies can also help conserve energy. Windows, however well weather stripped and sealed, are potential sites of heat loss in the winter and heat entry in summer. Heavy lined draperies can hold in the heat in the winter and keep the night coolness or air conditioning in your home in the summer. This will help your energy bills. Even unlined curtains can prevent outside air from entering your home. Keep this in mind when you plan your window treatments so that you can cover the entire window when you wish.

CARE OF WINDOW COVERINGS

The care of shades, blinds, curtains, and draperies is usually fairly simple. If you live in an area where the windows don't need to be washed more than about twice a year, you may want to clean your window coverings when you wash the windows. In most places, however, they will capture dust and should be cleaned about once a month.

Your vacuum cleaner, with the dusting attachment, is your best friend here. The vacuum should be used to clean not only your shades or Venetian blinds but also curtains, draperies, and whatever type of decorative heading you have.

Whether or not your curtains and draperies can also be washed depends on what they are made of and the trimmings on them.*

As a general rule, most curtains can be washed by machine, while many draperies must be dry cleaned.

Sheer and fragile curtains may survive machine washing better if they are inside a mesh bag. Curtains made of glass fiber should be washed by hand (be sure to protect your hands) to avoid getting slivers of glass in the washing machine.

Many man-made fiber curtains and draperies benefit from being hung at the window while still wet. Protect the floors from drips, of course.

*For specific information, see *The Butterick Fabric Handbook* (1975).

Information on selecting fabrics for curtains and draperies will be found in chapter 17, "Fabrics for Home Furnishings."

CURTAIN ROD RETURNS

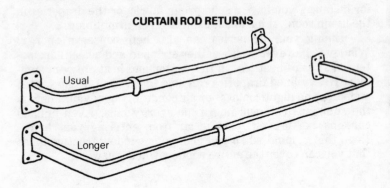

MEASURING WINDOWS FOR WINDOW TREATMENTS

Fullness is essential in getting the proper effect from curtains and draperies. Allow at least twice the measurement of the window for the fabric; for sheer fabrics, such as organdy, three times the window measurement is better. If hardware to be used with curtains or draperies extends fairly far out from window, include the return (area from point where rod begins to point where rod starts to parallel window) in measurements. Decide on curtain or drapery length before taking measurements.

Basic Considerations	Measuring
Glass curtains	Rod goes inside frame of window; measure width from inside frame to inside frame. Curtains reach windowsill; measure from just below top of window on inside of frame to sill, adding allowances for hems, rod casing.
Café curtains	As for glass curtains, but length goes to halfway down window; measurements begin again and continue to sill. May be changed as desired.
Draperies	Rod goes outside and above frame of window; install rod first, then measure, including return. Measure from top of rod to desired length and from side to side of rod, rather than of window; include allowance for fullness, extra fabric for hems, casing or pleating.
Repeats (width required for pattern)	Extra fabric is required to match pattern. Figure required fabric by length — if windows are 72″ long including hem allowance and fabric is 45″ wide with rod 40″, you will need two 72″ (six-foot) lengths — 144″, twelve feet, or four yards. If pattern repeats every nine inches, divide 144″ (inches needed) by nine. It comes out even (sixteen), so you need no extra fabric; if the answer were a fraction, you would have to buy enough extra fabric to pick up another entire repeat.

11

Fabrics for Home Furnishings

Fabrics for home furnishings form a large subdivision within the general world of fabrics. These fabrics should have certain characteristics. Ideally, they should wear well and be attractive, colorfast, and capable of being cleaned.

Certain additional fabric requirements should be met by fabrics to be used for upholstery, others by fabrics to be used for bedding, and still others for fabrics to be used for curtains and draperies. Rugs and carpets are covered in chapter 12, "Room Backgrounds."

GENERAL CONSIDERATIONS

Despite the different needs of home furnishings fabrics for different purposes there are certain general characteristics that should be considered before purchasing.

Among the most important is the fiber from which a particular fabric is made. The chart at the end of this chapter gives the characteristics of fibers most commonly used in home furnishings.

Unfortunately, a knowledge of the fibers themselves doesn't provide all the information you need. Many times you will find that a fabric is not made entirely of one fiber but is a blend of two or more fibers. This blending is done for various reasons. It can be for comfort (polyester, for instance, tends to feel cold, and blending it with cotton gives it a warmer feeling); appearance (acetate and rayon are sometimes blended with other fibers because of their ability to take color); or expense.

In buying a fabric for home furnishing, check to see what the dominant fiber is. The fabric will perform more or less in accordance with that fiber. Also notice if there are any weak fibers in the blend. Their weaknesses may interfere with the overall performance.

FABRIC COLORS

In addition to looking at fabric from the point of view of fiber, you should also consider its coloring. Color can cause problems with home furnishings both at the time of purchase and later.

One problem, more important with solid colors than with patterns, is inherent in making a purchase from a swatch, as you will do if you are buying upholstered furniture. The swatches (despite what the salesperson may tell you) should be considered approximations of color rather than the actual color. This is because it is difficult to avoid changing a color — even if only slightly — between one dyeing session and another. If you are planning to have two items covered with the same solid fabric, insist that the fabrics be taken from the same dye lot. *Dye lot* is the term for one session of dyeing. Get a promise in writing that this will be done.

Another problem is how long the color will last. This is determined to a large degree by the type of dye used and the dyeing method.

The terms *solution* or *dope dyed* mean that color is put into one of the man-made fibers while it is liquid, before it is formed into the fibers which are eventually made into the yarn which is finally made into cloth.

Vat dyeing is a somewhat confusing term. The important thing about vat dyeing isn't the vat but that the dyes are oxidized when they combine with the fiber. Both solution dyes and vat dyes are considered more colorfast than other dyes.

Whatever type of dyeing is used on your home furnishings fabrics, you should realize that any color will change over a period of time due to soil, light, oxidation, and such atmospheric conditions as sulphur in the air. The most that can be now achieved is a resistance to color change.

Certain colors tend to be more difficult to dye permanently than other colors. Blues and greens are in this category. Due to this difficulty, black fabrics often have a buildup of coloring. This is because black fabrics are often fabrics which were originally another color. When the first color failed to appear as desired by the manufacturer, it was hidden by being dyed black. Sniff at any black fabric before you buy it; it may have an offensive odor from layered dyes or from the actual black dye itself.

Certain fibers, too, present problems in either the dyeing of color or the fastness of it. Some fibers, too, especially acetate, are more affected by atmospheric conditions than others. Acetate, although it can be dyed in rich, glowing colors, is more likely to have a dramatic color change after exposure to atmosphere — from a fir green to an olive green, for instance — than cotton.

FABRICS FOR UPHOLSTERY

Fabrics for upholstered furniture are often pre-selected by the manufacturer. When choosing which one you want to use, keep in mind that there is a category on most furniture price labels which reads "C.O.M." This stands for customer's own material. You may find an upholstery fabric you prefer to those offered by the manufacturer in an upholstery fabric department.

Most upholstered furniture manufacturers offer a choice of fabrics for each piece of furniture. These will be shown to you in swatches. They are usually labeled (and the item priced) by grades — for example, Grade A, Grade B, and Grade C. Grade A is usually the most expensive fabric and Grade C the least expensive.

Keep in mind that there are many elements which determine the pricing of a fabric. Despite what the salesperson may tell you, it is perfectly possible for a Grade C fabric to wear better than a Grade A. Look at all the grades of fabric if you do not choose to use your own material.

Fabric prices may be more or less expensive because of fluctuations in the cost of the fibers. Synthetic and natural fiber prices are highly changeable. Synthetic fiber prices are often affected by petroleum prices, because many synthetics are petroleum derivatives. Natural fibers such as cotton are affected by natural events such as crop yields, and by demand. For these reasons, less durable fabrics may be more expensive than longer-lasting fabrics.

Hold any upholstery fabric you are considering up to the light. If you can see light through it, it is not woven closely enough to last longer than six months or so.

The design of a fabric can affect fabric price. If a fabric manufacturer can produce the same fabric year after year, as some upholstery fabric manufacturers do, the price will be lower than for a fabric produced only for six months.

In selecting an upholstery fabric, look for one which is tough and sturdy as well as being closely woven. Some knit fabrics are used for upholstered furniture, but these are relatively rare. If you are considering one, remember that the stitches should be close together even when the fabric is stretched.

Pay extra to have a soil-repellent finish added to any fabric you use for upholstery or slipcovers if it is not already treated in this way. These finishes should resist oil-based as well as water-based stains and will keep your upholstery looking clean much longer. If you buy a fabric which does not already have such a finish, you will notice that the finish darkens or yellows the fabric when it is applied. You might as well ignore this — without the finish, the fabric would darken, too, with dirt.

If you are familiar primarily with dress fabrics, you will have a pleasant surprise when you look at upholstery fabrics by the yard. These fabrics usually have their measurements given as "usable width of material." This means that if a fabric is labeled 45″ wide, for instance, there will be about an inch on either side of the 45″, including the selvage, so that it will actually measure 47″.

TYPES OF UPHOLSTERY FABRIC

Fabrics used in upholstery are usually of two types — flat weaves and pile fabrics. We mentioned that some knit fabrics are being suggested for upholstery. Knit slipcovers that stretch to fit onto furniture have proved popular but the upholstery fabrics are, as yet, very rare.

Flat weaves include such fabrics as damasks (this is a fabric with a pattern, usually in the same color, woven into it), satins, tweeds, and so forth. These weaves are made by yarns going under and over each other at right angles.

Pile fabrics include velvet and corduroy. Fabrics with a longer pile may be called *plush*. These have either loops or cut threads on their surface. Loops can be tricky; if they aren't woven tightly enough or if they are a little too long, they can snag and pull. Some pile fabrics, including the velvets and corduroys, can have the pile worn away with use. This results in a loss of good appearance. A strong synthetic fiber, such as nylon or polyester, can delay this.

FLOOR SAMPLES

Floor samples (furniture used for display purposes) and cancelled orders can often be sources of bargains when you are buying upholstered furniture.

Floor samples may be in somewhat undesirable colors because they are often part of a store's model rooms and therefore are covered in newsy rather than really desirable fabrics. If you see a real bargain in a floor sample but hate its upholstery, remember that you can always have slipcovers made or make them yourself.

Cancelled orders are either furniture that has been returned to the store by a customer or furniture for which the customer grew tired of waiting.

Most stores begin by reducing the price of floor samples and cancelled orders by 20 percent of the retail price. They will often offer additional markdowns, usually 10 percent at a time, if an item doesn't sell. Don't wait too long to buy a piece, however, in the hopes that it will go down to a very low price. Many stores prefer to give it to charity or save it for a "warehouse sale" rather than having unsalable merchandise on display.

BUYING READY-UPHOLSTERED FURNITURE

Some furniture comes already upholstered. Before buying such a piece, check the points listed here.

• The fabric should be placed so that the grain runs straight up and down the chair or sofa. The pattern designs should be matched where they meet (this may not always be possible, so see if it is offensive before rejecting the piece of furniture).

• Patterns, if large, should be centered on the back of the piece and on the cushions.

• Welting (covered cord that trims the seams of some furniture) should be made from a solid piece of fabric with few seams. It should appear neat.

• Run your hand over the furniture. The fabric should be smooth. There should be no wrinkles, and no puckers should form as your hand moves.

Good-quality seat cushions have concealed zippers (hidden under the fabric). There is some disagreement about the purpose of these zippers. Some experts say their purpose is only to permit you to straighten the cushion inside its fabric covering; they say cushions must be cleaned with the cushion in the cover. Furniture manufacturers, on the other hand, disagree. They say the zippers are so that the cushions can be taken out of their covers for cleaning. The answer? If the fabric is guaranteed not to shrink and you have that promise in writing, take the cushions out. Otherwise, don't risk it.

BED TICKING

The fabric which covers mattresses and box springs is called ticking. This was originally a closely woven linen or cotton fabric, usually striped, but today ticking is often printed with a pattern and sometimes is made of shiny plastic.

Most ticking fabrics are more than adequate for their job. If you object to one type of ticking or another — many people dislike slippery tickings — take that into consideration.

The ticking is mainly designed to contain and protect the materials from which a mattress or box spring is made. When mattresses were made largely of feathers and down, ticking held in the feathers. You will occasionally see the term "downproof ticking" used. This means that the ticking is woven closely enough to prevent feathers and down from sifting through. Although it is unimportant today, it is an indication of a closely woven fabric, a desirable quality.

Ticking can be tufted, smooth, or quilted. Again, which you prefer is a personal matter. On foam mattresses, ticking which is attached somehow to the foam will help prevent it from slipping.

Although ticking is only a finishing touch and the pattern is hidden by the bedclothes, mattresses and box springs can often be bought at bargain prices because the ticking has been discontinued, that is, no longer made by the manufacturer. If a mattress or box spring with discontinued ticking has other features you want, buying it is definitely to your advantage.

SOFA BEDS

Sofa bed fabrics present special problems. This is because these fabrics and the sofa bed itself receive so much use. Although you can occasionally use a relatively lightweight fabric for an infrequently used chair (a dining room side chair, for instance), it is essential that any fabric covering double-duty sleeping-sitting furniture be sturdy and strong. Choose a closely woven fabric with a soil-repellent finish.

CURTAIN AND DRAPERY FABRICS

Fabrics used for draperies are often identical to upholstery fabrics. Curtain fabrics are usually lighter in weight.

Because curtains and draperies are not subject to as much wear as upholstery (no one sits on them) the fabrics can be more loosely woven. Most curtain and drapery fabrics are woven. Some curtain fabrics now available are made by a method usually called sewing-knitting or Malimo, from the best-known machine that makes this type of fabric. These fabrics are very open in appearance. Glass fibers are often used for curtains and draperies. Glass has strength and good resistance to sunlight, but is affected by abrasion. See the chart in this chapter for characteristics of different fibers.

CARE OF HOME FURNISHINGS FABRICS

The care of home furnishings fabrics is complicated by the fact that many different fabrics are used and they are often used in combination with other elements, as is the case with upholstery. Nevertheless, here are some general care rules:

• Use the vacuum cleaner regularly on all home furnishings fabrics. This is better than using a brush because brushing can wear away or damage some of the fabric. You may find, however, that your vacuum cleaner doesn't pick up all the soil. This is most likely to be a problem with electrostatic furniture (likely to be either covered with a synthetic fabric or made from a synthetic plastic). In such a case, use a whisk broom to remove soil.

• Cushions on upholstered furniture should be turned to distribute the wear. Not all cushions, however, are designed to be used on both sides, in which case this step must be omitted.

• If you have down- or feather-filled cushions, be sure they are inside a downproof fabric before vacuum cleaning. If feathers sift out through the cushions when you plump them, the ticking is not downproof enough to use a vacuum, since vacuuming will draw out additional feathers and down.

• Vacuuming should also be done regularly to clean bedding upholstery and curtains and draperies.

• Upholstered furniture can be shampooed. This is more difficult than is usually admitted, takes a long time (the furniture needs to dry), and is not always completely satisfactory. Use either a cleaner which is especially made for shampooing furniture or make your own from detergent (not soap) and warm water. Beat it with an egg beater to get foam. The foam is what is said to do the cleaning. Put foam on the furniture with a sponge. Cover a small area at a time and clean in circles. Remove the suds with a dry sponge or a towel. If your upholstery has a soil-repellent finish it is especially important to get all the suds off the furniture — the left-on suds can harm the finish. Go over the upholstery once again with a clean cloth or sponge which has been dipped in warm water and wrung out. Open the windows and turn on a fan or the air conditioner. This is to dry the furniture as quickly as possible.

• Fabrics which are not colorfast, are likely to shrink, or are labeled as being dry-cleanable only can, in theory, be dry cleaned at home. Don't try this on foam furniture — the fluid may dissolve the foam. Put the cleaning agent on with a sponge or cloth. Clean quickly. Always, of course, read the label for safety for you and your furniture. Any dry-cleaning fluid tends to be extremely dangerous. When these things aren't highly flammable, they are likely to cause permanent liver damage. This is why we do not recommend dry cleaning except, perhaps, with one of the powder cleaners. Read the labels carefully.

• Professional cleaning of home furnishings items is widely available. In many cases, this is the best solution to the dirt problem.

Several charts follow. They include a chart giving the amount of fabric needed to upholster or slipcover the average piece of upholstered furniture, a chart giving fabric required for bedspreads for various kinds of beds, a chart of commonly found home furnishings fibers, a chart on care, and a stain removal chart.

FABRIC REQUIREMENTS FOR UPHOLSTERING OR SLIPCOVERING

Following is a chart of yardage requirements for upholstering or slipcovering some of the most common pieces of furniture. The requirements are estimates, although on the generous side; if your furniture is either large or smaller the requirements will change accordingly. The estimates given are for solid fabrics and fabrics with small all-over prints or patterns. Large, splashy prints will require additional fabric. Measurements are for fabric at least 48″ wide.

Furniture	Number of Cushions	Yards Needed
6- to 7-foot sofas	3	16
	1	15
	0	12
Love seat	1	11
	0	10
Armchair	1	8½
	0	7½
Sofa bed	2	15
Chaise longue	2	12
	1	11
	0	9
Ottoman (measure carefully — sizes vary)		2

BEDSPREAD FABRIC REQUIREMENTS

Bed	Finished Spread Size	Yards of 45″ Fabric Needed
Single	75″ x 108″	6 yards
Twin	81″ x 108″	6 yards
Full (double)	96″ x 108″	6 yards
Queen	102″ x 120″	8 yards
King	114″ x 120″	8 yards

Bed sizes are not truly standardized; measure your beds before buying fabric. Included in the above figures is a measurement of 21″ as the height of the bed from the floor. This measurement may vary, too. All spreads extend to just above the floor.

FIBERS USED COMMONLY FOR HOME FURNISHINGS FABRICS

For more complete information and understanding, see the *Butterick Fabric Handbook*. Blends of more than one fiber should be viewed as the weakest fiber in the blend, although often stronger fibers will reduce disadvantages of weaker.

Fiber	Color Fastness	Abrasion Resistance	Durability	Use
Acetate	Takes color well but may be affected by atmospheric fumes	Weaker than average	Weaker than average; weakened by sunlight	Draperies, some upholstery
Acrylic	May darken	Good	Tends to pill; resists sunlight	Upholstery, draperies
Cotton	Affected by sunlight	Good	Good, but shrinks unless treated; wrinkles easily unless treated	All decorative uses
Glass	Excellent	May crack	Extremely durable except for cracking; care should be taken in handling to avoid glass splinters	Curtains almost exclusively
Linen	Certain colors may run or fade	May show wear at edges	Good durability; shrinks unless treated; wrinkles easily unless treated	All decorative uses

Fiber				
Modacrylic	May darken	Good	Extremely sensitive to heat	Fake furs, pile fabrics, rugs and upholstery
Nylon	Pale colors may fade	Excellent	Fades in sunlight	Curtains, upholstery, rugs
Olefin	Good	Good	Strong fiber; fast drying but heat sensitive	Upholstery, rugs
Polyester	Good	Excellent	Excellent; may pill or attract lint; most versatile man-made fiber	All decorative uses
Rayon	Solution- (dope-) dyed; colorfast	Weaker than average	Weaker than most and affected by sunlight; high wet-modulus and high tenacity rayons are stronger than other types	All decorative uses
Saran	Good	Good	Stiff; softens at relatively low temperature	Outdoor furniture
Silk	May change or run	Good	Weakened by sunlight but the ultimate luxury fabric for home furnishings	All decorative uses, rugs rarely
Wool	Good	Good	Shrinks; attractive to moths unless treated	All decorative uses, draperies rarely

CARE OF FIBERS USED FOR HOME FURNISHINGS

Generally speaking, most curtains can be washed; most draperies and slipcovers are better dry cleaned. If you are making your own curtains and plan to wash them, wash them once before making them. This way shrinkage should not be a further problem. Upholstered furniture can be cleaned as described in the text; for anything more elaborate, a professional should be used.

Fiber	Care	Special Instructions
Acetate	Dry clean	Acetone and a few other chemicals destroy acetate; be careful with nail polish remover, drugs
Acrylic	Wash by hand in warm water	
Cotton	Machine wash in hot water	Be sure colors are fast first; if color runs, have item dry cleaned
Glass fibers	Wash by hand, drip dry	Take care to avoid getting glass slivers in hands
Linen	Dry clean to preserve dark colors; light colors may be machine washed	
Modacrylic	Have pile fabric dry cleaned	
Nylon	Machine wash, tumble dry	
Olefin	Machine wash in lukewarm water, dry at lowest machine setting	Badly affected by heat; never iron
Polyester	Machine wash, warm; dry at low; remove from dryer promptly to avoid permanent wrinkles	Avoid over-drying
Rayon	Dry clean	

Fiber	Care	Special Instructions
Saran	Sponge or hose clean	
Silk	Dry clean	
Vinyl	Sponge	
Wool	Dry clean	

STAIN REMOVAL CHART

Stain	Removal Method
Ballpoint pen ink	Ballpoint pen ink comes out quite easily when sponged with rubbing alcohol. On a washable fabric, any stain which remains should be rubbed with soap or a detergent and then the fabric should be washed. The same method should be used on non-washable items, followed by sponging with a mild detergent solution of 1 teaspoon detergent to 1 cup of water.
Blood	Washable fabrics should be soaked in cold water immediately. If they do not respond to cold water, an enzyme pre-soak (when available) should be used. The fabrics should then be washed in the usual way. Non-washable items should be sponged with cold water followed by a mild detergent solution (1 teaspoon detergent to 1 cup of water). If the detergent solution doesn't work, try a solution of 1 tablespoon ammonia in a cup of water — and if that changes the color of the item, follow it up by sponging with ¼ cup white vinegar in 1 cup of water to bring back the original color. Test both the ammonia solution and the vinegar solution in some inconspicuous spot before using on the stain.
Candle wax	Follow instructions for chewing gum, below.
Chewing gum	Chewing gum can be removed from most fabrics if it is first hardened by rubbing it with an ice cube and then scraped off with a blunt knife or your fingernail. This takes time and patience but it does work. In desperate cases, you can try sponging the gum with a non-flammable cleaning fluid, but this can spread the stain.

Stain	Removal Method
Coffee, tea	Simple washing will usually remove coffee and tea stains on washable fabrics. On non-washable fabrics, sponge with cold water first, then try mild detergent solution of 1 teaspoon detergent to 1 cup of water.
Cream, milk	Washing will remove cream and milk from washable fabrics. On non-washable fabrics, start by wiping with a damp sponge. If that fails, shake cornstarch or white talcum powder onto the stain, allow to dry thoroughly, then use a brush or vacuum to remove the residue.
Greasy stains, including lipstick, tar	Start by following the ice-cube method given for chewing gum, then use lighter fluid to remove remaining stain on both washable and non-washable fabrics.
Nail polish	Nail polish remover will remove nail polish from most fabrics, but NEVER use it on acetate or triacetate. On these fabrics, try to scrape the polish off with a blunt knife or fingernail.
Paint (oil based)	See instructions for nail polish, above.
Paint (water based)	If the paint is still wet, sponge with water, trying not to spread the stain further. If the paint is dry, nothing (including dry cleaning) will get it out, but you may be able to scrape some off the surface with a blunt knife or your fingernail.
Perspiration	Certain man-made fibers seem to hold perspiration odors longer than other fabrics; although a stain will come out with washing, the odor may not. Rub the area of the odor with a deodorant soap before washing.
Urine, vomit, mucous	On washable fabrics, soak in an enzyme pre-soak (if possible) then wash using a suitable bleach (chlorine or oxygen type). On non-washable items, such as rugs, sponge first with mild detergent solution (1 teaspoon detergent to a cup of water) and rinse. If that doesn't work, try white vinegar solution — ¼ cup white vinegar to 1 cup water. If this solution changes the color, try to neutralize it with an ammonia solution of 1 tablespoon ammonia to 1 cup water. Test both the ammonia solution and the vinegar solution in an inconspicuous spot before using on the stain.

12

Room Backgrounds

The background of a room, almost as much as the furniture itself, sets the mood of a room and tells something about the people who live in it. The "background of a room" as referred to here means the walls, floors, and ceiling.

At one time, decorating was limited to putting rugs on floors, white paint on ceilings, and wallpaper on walls. Today, however, as we become more adventurous, we're realizing that sometimes the paint might be better on the floor, the carpet on the wall, and the wallpaper on the ceiling.

Room background affects not only the mood and the appearance of a room, but also the way sounds resonate in a room. A room which is too "live" will have echoes which make voices seem unnecessarily and annoyingly shrill. A room which is too "dead" will muffle sounds. This can be soothing but may make it difficult to understand conversation and may dull musical sounds.

SETTING A MOOD

The mood set by a room background can be formal, informal, or any variation in between. Other elements, including

WALL GRAPHIC

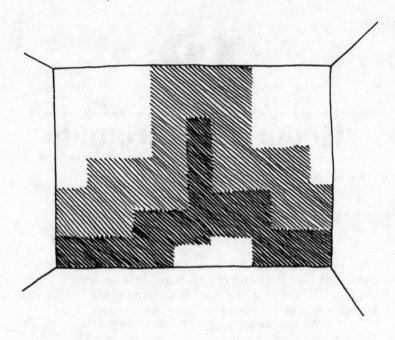

the furniture, contribute to it, but backgrounds are perhaps most important. The points listed below only apply generally. There are always exceptions.

• Primary or very vibrant colors tend to be less formal than most subtle colors. Large wall graphics (geometric forms in color) also tend to be informal.

• Dark colors and very subtle colors tend to be more formal. Extremely regular designs in wallpaper or rugs, especially when done in colors such as gold on white, are more formal than less regular designs.

• Panelling, usually wood or plastic made to look like wood, can be formal or informal. Dark woods or white-painted woods usually create a more informal effect than light natural wood.

CONTROLLING SOUND

The science of sound, also called acoustics, is complicated, but the aspects of it that apply to decorating in the home are basic enough to work with. Here are some generally accepted rules you can follow.

A room should be neither too live nor too dead. Most rooms are too live. Liveness and deadness are determined by the way sound echoes in a room.

Liveness is caused by sounds bouncing off a flat surface. Because most rooms are built so that sound waves have many flat surfaces to bounce off, an ordinary rectangular room is very live, especially when unfurnished. A round room is much deader than a rectangular one.

Too live a room can be deadened by replacing or covering sound-reflecting materials with sound-absorbing ones. A rug on a wood or tile floor muffles the sound reflecting from that surface. Books have excellent sound-muffling qualities; a bookcase wall will muffle sound. Curtains and draperies muffle the sound from window walls.

If a room is still too live after it is furnished, look for a large, flat, hard-surfaced expanse in it. Try covering this with a blanket to see if it helps. If it does, consider carpeting if it's a floor or a wall, suspended fabric for a wall or a ceiling, or acoustic tiling for a ceiling.

USING PAINT

Paint is one popular way to create a room background. Paint is used on more surfaces in more rooms for more reasons than anything else. Paint, as we mentioned in the chapter on color, texture, and pattern, is one of the cheapest and easiest ways to get a quick effect. It is used on walls, woodwork, floors, and ceilings.

Paint comes in various types and finishes. Speaking broadly, there are two types of paint — enamel, which is shiny, and flat, which is dull.

Decorating tradition has it that woodwork paint — the paint on doors, door frames, window sills, and so forth — should be glossy. This is because glossy paint is easier to clean and has a more durable surface than dull paint.

Other rules apply to walls. One rule says that all wall paints should be flat. Another says that all light-colored wall paints should be dull, all dark-colored wall paints glossy. The theory behind the rules is that the light colors don't need to be brightened by reflecting additional light, while the dark colors need as much light bounced off them as possible. In practice, most people use dull paints on walls and glossy paint for woodwork.

There used to be a limited choice of paint types. There were oil-based paints and water-based paints and that was it. Today, however, paints have changed, and various developments have made the choice of paints both wider and somewhat more confusing.

For room walls and ceilings, many people choose an interior latex paint. Latex is a flat paint which dries quickly and comes off brushes or rollers with ordinary detergent and water. Most of the flat paints now available tend to come out of their cans looking quite thick, somewhat like clotted cream. They go on easily with a roller or a brush (a roller usually gives a smoother surface), and there is rarely much of a problem from the paint dripping. Although the brushes and rollers can be cleaned easily, spilled paint can be a problem. If it dries and hardens, it is almost impossible to remove.

PAINTING THE WALLS

Whether you decide to paint a room yourself or to have a professional painter come in to do it, take as much as possible from the room to create space to work. Any furniture left in the room — and the floor — should be covered with drop cloths, which can be bought in a paint supply store. Take all hardware (switch plates and so forth) off the walls and ceiling.

If you decide to paint a room yourself, begin by stripping in the edges. Stripping in means going along the edges where the wall joins the ceiling and floors and painting a two- to three-inch border with a brush or edging tool. This ensures that the corners will be covered.

You will probably want to use both a brush and a roller if you paint a room yourself. Stripping in is easier with a brush or edging tool; painting a large area is easier with a roller.

Use a paint tray with the roller. Pour paint from the can

into the tray, move the roller back and forth through the paint in the tray, and then apply the paint with the roller to the surface being painted.

Start rolling on the paint by making large zigzags on a space about nine square feet (three feet by three feet, for example). Working one direction only, cover the entire wall, going over the zigzags. Smooth out uneven paint, but don't make the covering too thin.

ZIGZAG PAINTING

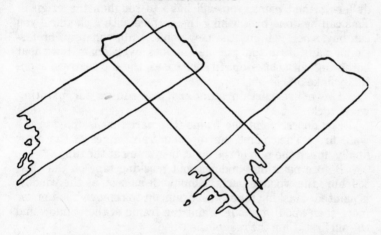

A gallon of paint covers about 500 square feet. See the chart at the end of this chapter for how to determine square footage. If you plan to give a room two coats of paint you will of course need twice as much paint as if you plan to give it one coat.

Until recently, light colors usually needed two coats to cover what was on the wall, dark colors one coat. The dark colors gained their opacity through the use of a lead base. For safety reasons (lead is poisonous if ingested) lead-based paints are no longer sold in the United States. Dark-color paints currently produced have new non-lead-based formulations, so even two coats of some dark colors may not cover.

Some experts recommend that a white opaque base coat be applied before using one of the darker colors. It may be worth testing a small area to see if this is necessary for the color you have chosen. In any case, any paint job looks better with two coats. Whether you decide to use one or two depends on how high your standards are.

PAINTING WOODWORK AND FLOORS

Woodwork is usually painted with enamel. If you have enamel on your woodwork now and want to change to a duller-finished paint, you will have to roughen the original. This can be done by washing the surface with a chemical you can buy when you buy the new paint. Unfortunately, professional painters often put dull paints over enamel without bothering with this step. In such cases, the top coat will eventually flake off.

There are certain standard procedures for painting woodwork.

For doors, paint the frame (the part that is fixed to the wall) first. Then paint the top and front edges of the door; finally, finish the rest of the door, beginning at the top.

Before painting windows, put masking tape on the glass touching the wooden parts. Remove it as soon as the window is painted. Masking tape is very difficult to remove if left on for more than about an hour. Paint the frame of the window and the sill first, then the rest of the wood.

Paint can also be used quite successfully on floors. Old wood floors can be painted to hide a multitude of scratches, dents, and so forth. Concrete floors can be painted to both hold down dust and give a more finished look to the floor.

For the most elegant-looking painted floor, use a high gloss black or very deep brown paint such as deck paint.

For a more informal interior, consider a spatter dash floor. Use a glossy color for the base — dark colors or deep red seem to look best — and several small cans of enamel in various colors. Paint the floor a solid color with the base paint. Then, when the paint has dried, dip a brush into one of the enamels and hit the brush with a stick to spatter the color all over the floor. Use a different brush for each color but do all the spattering at one time. This can only be done, of course, in a room which can be kept empty until the paint dries. Finish up with a coat of one of the synthetic varnishes.

As a general rule, always paint surfaces you are using enamel on first, then surfaces where you are using a flat paint. Flat paint can be removed from enamel more easily than enamel from flat paint.

Read all instructions on paint cans. Because paint formulas change extremely rapidly, many old rules and theories no longer hold true. The instructions will usually give you good, up-to-date information.

USING WALLPAPER

Most of the time wallpaper is put on walls, although we will discuss placing it elsewhere. Like paint, it gives an immediate effect and is good, especially if definitely patterned, at covering up irregularities in walls.

The term *wall covering* is currently used for anything applied to a wall in the same way as wallpaper. The new term is used because paper is not always what these wall coverings are made of. In this discussion, unless we indicate otherwise, when we say wallpaper we are also referring to non-paper wall coverings such as the vinyls.

Wallpaper is usually made of paper, printed and sometimes also embossed in a pattern. It comes in various widths depending on the width of the pattern. No matter what the width of the wallpaper may be, a roll always covers thirty-five square feet. Some wallpapers are sold in double or triple rolls only. A double roll covers seventy square feet, a triple roll 105 square feet.

Most wallpaper is applied to the wall with wallpaper paste. At one time these pastes were natural glues, but since the natural substances tended to attract various kinds of insects that liked to eat the paste, synthetic glues were developed. Wallpaper pastes are almost always thinned with water.

HANGING WALLPAPER

To apply wallpaper, cut the paper into strips, leaving each strip longer than the area of the wall it will cover and allowing for matching the pattern. Matching the pattern is essential with wallpaper.

You will need a bucket in which to mix the wallpaper paste. Follow the instructions on the package of paste for how much water to add.

Remove all hardware such as switchplates from the wall.

Most experts suggest that you put up (hang) wallpaper by cutting the strips, covering the backs with glue, then lifting them and placing them on the wall.

This means you need a large table for applying the paste and nimble hands so that as you fold the paper in preparation for lifting it, it doesn't get stuck to itself and tear. This folding is usually done by bringing the two ends of the paper to the center of the strip and lifting the paper from the table. It is then positioned on the wall, middle first.

Actually, this complicated method of hanging wallpaper is not necessary.

Instead, a coat of paste can be applied to the wall with a brush. The paper, previously cut to the proper length, is then applied directly on the wall.

Wallpaper paste stays wet for some time so you can slide the paper around to adjust its position. When the wallpaper is positioned correctly, smooth it and trim the edges with a single-edged razor blade before the paste is dry.

VINYL WALL COVERINGS

Vinyl wall coverings have become extremely popular in recent years. They have the advantage of being scrubbable, so they are especially good for use in kitchens, bathrooms, children's rooms, and other places which get dirty quickly. Some vinyl wall coverings, with or without paper backing, are quite thick. Even so, you can hang them with ordinary wallpaper paste, or you can buy a wallpaper paste especially made for vinyl wallpapers.

Very thin vinyl wall covering already has adhesive on it. It has a paper backing which is peeled off before the wall covering is applied to the wall. The covering tends to stick to itself because of its adhesive back, but it can be pulled apart. This is hung in the same way as wallpaper, although because the patterns are usually smaller, matching patterns can be easier than with the usual wallpapers. This covering is sold by the yard and is carried in many stores such as hardware and ten-cent stores which don't stock other wall coverings.

STRIPPABLE WALLPAPER

This type of wallpaper can be removed from the wall by loosening one corner and then yanking swiftly.

In theory, this is a great idea. In practice, you may find that some of the wall comes away with the paper and some of the glue remains on the wall. It is easier, however, to remove strippable wallpaper than non-strippable wallpaper. To do that, use a special scraping tool after soaking the paper with a special solution.

PREPASTED WALLPAPER

Prepasted wallpapers are usually made with a dry paste on their backs. These papers must be put in water to activate the paste before being applied to the wall. The paper can be submerged in a bucket, a tub of water, or a special water holder designed for this purpose.

OTHER WALL COVERING IDEAS

Fabric is becoming an increasingly popular wall covering. Special pastes are available for putting fabrics on walls. Be sure that any fabric you select for the wall is colorfast so the colors won't run when the paste is applied. It should also be closely woven so that the wall won't show through.

Should you put new wallpaper over old? In theory, no. In practice, maybe. Make a few tests first.

• Hold the new wallpaper over the old to see if the old wallpaper shows through. If it does, you will either have to paint the wall or remove the old paper before putting on new wallpaper.

• The colors on the face of some wallpapers "bleed" (seep) when they meet with wallpaper glue or paint. To prevent your running into this trouble, test the effect of glue or paint on the old wallpaper. If, after the substance has been on for, say, an hour, the color doesn't smear when you rub your finger across it, you can assume the paper won't bleed.

OTHER USES FOR WALLPAPERS

Wallpaper can be used in other places besides the walls.

Wallpapered ceilings were common about fifty years ago; the papers usually had small white-on-white designs. Today, if wallpaper is used on a ceiling at all, it is not to make the ceiling white. Instead, it can be used very effectively in a room to give an enclosed and cosy feeling. A flowered wallpaper, for example, might be carried across the ceiling of a dining room, or a leafy paper could cover the walls and ceiling of a bedroom.

Matching can be difficult on ceilings. A pattern having an obvious one-way direction should be applied so that the direction of the pattern changes in the middle of the room.

Recently, some decorating magazines have shown wallpapered floors. These floors usually have tilelike wallpapers on them. The paper is put on the floor with wallpaper paste and then covered with many coats of clear synthetic varnish. The idea is novel but probably not really practical, because floors usually get such wear and tear. It could, however, work in a rarely used area such as the floor of a bay window used only for plants and a bird cage.

USING WOOD

Wood is used for room backgrounds, too. It is used for flooring, both in the narrow strips of the average house and in parquet patterns, for walls, and occasionally for ceilings.

Wood can be either elegant or casual, formal or informal, depending on the way it is used.

We have already discussed painting woodwork. In this section we shall begin by discussing the various types of wood molding and go on to discuss other uses of wood.

MOLDINGS

Some people believe moldings were originally designed to disguise the fact that it is very difficult to get a room square at the corners.

During the 1930s, 1940s, and into the 1950s believers in modern design advocated the elimination of molding. Decorators advised clients to rip off all the molding in their rooms for a fresh, open appearance. Recently those lines, once considered "clean," have come to be considered boxlike or characterless. Today, both home and professional decorators are keeping lumberyards and home centers happy by buying all kinds of molding to add to rooms.

What are the kinds of molding?

• The *baseboard* is the wood that runs along the bottom of a wall between the floor and the wall. It can keep spatters from cleaning (the floor, for instance) from reaching the wall covering, which is usually relatively fragile.

MOLDINGS

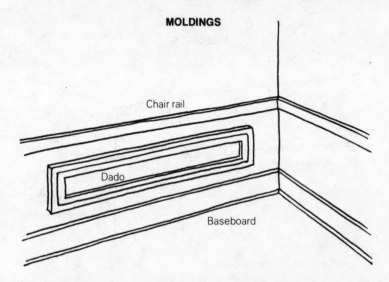

Chair rail

Dado

Baseboard

Baseboards are usually painted with glossy enamel, but they can be covered with tiles. Tiles give a nice effect and are also practical.

• A *dado* is similar to a baseboard but goes farther up the wall. It is often a nice compromise between an entire wood-panelled wall and a non-panelled wall.

A dado should be stained to bring out the color of the wood, or painted as was American colonial style.

If you like the look of a dado but feel you cannot afford a wood one, you can paint the lower part of the wall a different color from the top and use a strip of narrow molding to break up this space. You can also find wallpapers printed to look like wood dados.

The molding at the top of a dado is often called a *chair rail*. A separate piece of molding placed at this level is also a chair rail. A chair rail is positioned to keep chairs which are placed against the wall from hitting and marring the wall.

• Moving up the wall, the next type of molding is called a *picture rail* or *picture molding*. This juts into the room just below the ceiling and has a rounded top edge. Onto this are hung large curved hooks from which picture wire or an attractive rope is hung to support a picture.

MOLDINGS

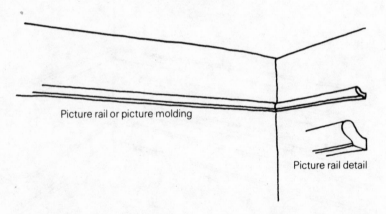

Picture rail or picture molding

Picture rail detail

Picture rails were designed to protect walls from being marred by hooks and nails for hanging pictures. They are still common in school and dormitory rooms.

In older houses with high ceilings, picture rails were usually placed about a foot below the ceiling. They minimize the height of a room and add architectural detailing even if pictures are not hung from them.

• The space between the picture rail and the ceiling is called a *cornice*. The word *cornice* is also used for the space between a chair rail and the floor and for a molded decorative section just below and parallel to the ceiling.

In rooms with high ceilings, this space can be painted the same color as the ceiling in order to lower the room.

WOOD PANELLING

Wood-panelled rooms are traditional and can be either formal or informal. The formal rooms are seen mainly in museums. These rooms have elaborately carved moldings and panelling with beautifully matched wood grains. Less formal rooms are usually built with prepared panelling available at lumberyards and home centers. A room can be panelled in any wood, and its formality is determined somewhat by the choice of wood. Pecky cypress, for instance, is less formal than cherry.

FURRING STRIP

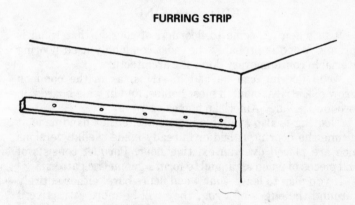

Wood panelling can be nailed directly to the wall if the walls aren't extremely irregular. If they are, furring strips (strips of wood) should be placed around the edges of the room and the panelling nailed to them.

WOOD CEILINGS

Attractively patterned wood can make extremely handsome ceilings. Like panelling, wood for ceilings can be bought from lumberyards and home centers and installed fairly easily.

Exposed beams — lengths of wood which support the building but are not hidden within the ceiling — are occasionally found on the ceilings of old houses. Beams may be added to newer homes to give an old-fashioned look.

WOOD IMITATIONS

All these types of wood have their imitations in wallpaper and synthetics. Some are more successful than others, so you will have to look around to see if what you want is one of the better results.

There are wood-pattern printed wallpapers and woodlike thick plastics for panelling a room. There are thinner woodlike plastic wall coverings suitable for the same purpose.

Imitation wood beams come in lightweight plastic. These are light enough so that they don't risk putting too great a strain on the ceiling.

WOOD FLOORING

It is when we come to flooring, of course, that wood is supreme. Wood is probably the most commonly used flooring material in contemporary domestic architecture.

Wood flooring can be laid in strips, as in the common narrow oak strips found in most homes, and in wide boards, in reproduction early American homes.

Flooring is also available in parquet, either handmade at the time the flooring is laid or in ready-made tilelike versions which are placed over an existing floor. Parquet consists of small pieces of wood arranged to form a geometric pattern.

If you plan to leave your wood floors bare, either entirely or around the edges of a rug, they will be more attractive if they are first sanded, then perhaps stained if the present color is unattractive, and finally sealed with one of the synthetic floor lacquers. These lacquers give the floors a shine, protect them from most spills, and eliminate the need for waxing.

Floors which do not have a strong finish on them should be waxed to protect the surface. Paste wax, applied in a thin coat and then buffed, is the best wax to use, but a liquid floor wax goes on easier. Do not use one of the self-polishing waxes made for vinyl; there are certain chemicals in such waxes which may dissolve the finish.

RUGS AND CARPETS

Carpet is the general term — it includes rugs. Carpets are usually found on the floor and on stairs, but may on occasion cover walls, usually to improve the acoustics in a too-live room, or to give the illusion of a larger room.

Strictly speaking, the words *rug* and *carpet* can be used interchangeably. In recent years, however, they have come to have different meanings.

• A carpet usually fastens to and covers the entire floor.

• A rug usually does not cover the entire floor and is not fastened down.

• The term *area rug* is used to describe a rug, usually dramatic in pattern, color, or texture (such as the long, shaggy rya rugs from Scandinavia), which is either used on top of carpeting or alone. Area rugs are often used to set off one section of a room from the rest of the room. Oriental and Persian rugs can be considered area rugs.

WALL-TO-WALL CARPETING

There is controversy over whether wall-to-wall carpeting or rugs are more effective and useful. Here are some points to consider before making your decision.

• Wall-to-wall carpeting extends the apparent space in a home. If used throughout the home in the same color, wall-to-wall carpeting gives the impression that the rooms flow into each other.

• Traffic patterns may show up on wall-to-wall carpeting, and because wall-to-wall carpeting is fixed to the floor, it can't be turned to equalize the wear.

• For the same reason, wall-to-wall carpeting must usually be cleaned professionally while it's on the floor. Rugs can be sent out for cleaning.

• Wall-to-wall carpeting is often difficult to move from one house or apartment to another because of size differences. It can always be cut up, bound, and turned into rugs, however.

• Wall-to-wall carpeting is more expensive than a rug since it must be cut to fit and there is a certain amount of waste, but it can give a luxurious look to a home.

• Wall-to-wall carpeting has traditionally been used in solid colors. Today, there is a trend toward greater pattern variety throughout the home. Rugs provide this more easily than carpeting.

CHOOSING RUGS AND CARPETS

Here are highlights of the most important points to take into consideration in choosing floor coverings.

• Both natural and man-made fibers are used for rugs and carpets. The man-made fibers absorb moisture slowly, are non-allergenic, are not affected by mildew, and resist moths and other insects.

However, these fibers tend to build up static electricity (you can get a shock after walking on them). Special rug and carpet finishing processes can reduce this; commercial anti-static products are also available which you can apply yourself.

• In choosing rug color, keep in mind that medium shades show dirt less quickly than dark or light shades. Patterned rugs and carpets look clean longer than solid rugs and carpets do. Recently, tweed rugs, combining three colors or three tones of one color, have been introduced. These are excellent at hiding dirt.

• Texture is also an important consideration in choosing a rug. Bear in mind that it affects not only the look of the rug and the room but also its wearing ability.

The surface of the carpet, called the pile, can be one of the most important considerations in selecting carpet. Plush, for instance, is a thick, luxurious pile, fine for a formal room which gets little traffic but probably wrong for a hallway or a family living room in which many children will play in a small space. The carpet fibers and types chart at the end of this chapter gives more information about wearing qualities.

• Buy a pad (sometimes called a cushion or underlay) when you buy a carpet or rug. Padding will both lengthen the life of your carpet and make it more comfortable to walk on.

• When you buy carpeting for stairs, buy a little extra. This can be folded over at the end and when the carpet begins to wear along the edges of the stairs, this can be moved up or down and the entire carpet shifted.

• As rugs again become vibrant and colorful, more and more rugs are ending up on the wall. Sometimes families hook their own, intending to use them on the floor, then find they're so beautiful that the wall is the best place to show them off.

These rugs do more than just add a decorative note to a wall. They also serve to lessen the "liveness" of a room and add insulation — an important consideration for energy saving.

RUG AND CARPET CARE

Clean rugs and carpets by regular vacuuming. Some people prefer upright vacuum cleaners, but tank types are perfectly acceptable. A carpet sweeper or a broom can be used for surface cleaning when you don't have time to vacuum. Rug cleaning compounds and machines are available to buy or to rent; unfortunately, these are somewhat difficult to use and do not, as yet, equal professional cleaning.

RESILIENT FLOORING

Resilient flooring is the name given to such floor coverings as sheet or tile vinyl flooring. These floor coverings are often fixed to the floor with an adhesive. This means the surface underneath should be as smooth as possible and that manufacturers' instructions for installation should be followed.

Sheet flooring is easier to lay than tile flooring, as it goes down almost in one step. Tile flooring may, however, be more economical if the shape of your room means that many zigs and zags must be made in the covering.

Almost every type of resilient flooring comes in either sheet or tile form. If you find a pattern you like in one form and not the other, your decision is more or less made for you.

There is always the possibility that water or other liquids will seep under these floorings. This is more likely to happen with tiles than with sheeting because the former has more seams.

Here is a listing of the types of resilient flooring available.

• *Asphalt tile* is low in cost but can be damaged by both grease and petroleum-based products (certain paints, for instance). Asphalt tile is quiet but is subject to cracks. It is not available in great quantity for homes now.

• *Linoleum* is the old standby floor covering, now somewhat difficult to find as the vinyls have become more popular. It resists grease but not alkaline substances such as lye. Be sure whatever you use to clean it is suitable for linoleum. Linoleum benefits from waxing. Avoid installing it on concrete which is directly over the ground — it tends to get musty.

• *Vinyl-asbestos* tile is moderately priced and easy to care for. (Clean by washing, with or without waxing.)

• *Homogenous vinyl* is also available in tile form and comes in many types, from custom designs (your name, for instance) to the self-sticking tiles with peel-off paper backing. Clean by washing, with or without waxing.

• *Cushioned vinyl* has a foam backing. This overcomes to some extent one of the objections to vinyl floorings — they tend to be tiring to stand on for any length of time. Clean by washing, with or without waxing.

• *Roto vinyl* is relatively inexpensive. It has a base of asbestos or felt, a layer of vinyl, a printed pattern, and a vinyl topping. It is fairly satisfactory but the top layer may eventually wear off and, of course, the pattern may follow.

• *Inlaid vinyl* is vinyl in which the pattern and the color go through the vinyl. Pattern does not wear away as with roto vinyl.

The vinyl floorings are resistant to grease, other spills, alkalis. They are not resistant to heat — don't put a hot pan on your vinyl floor, because it can melt.

The thicker the vinyl, the better it is and the more expensive it will be. Patterns imitate almost anything in nature or the imagination — parquet wood flooring, bricks, antique tiles. Some sort of pattern is recommended as this helps the floor to remain clean looking longer.

Vinyl does make a room more "live" than almost any other floor, including wood. If you find you are annoyed by the sound once you have a vinyl floor, consider adding sound-deadening items to the rest of the room.

All vinyl flooring can be cleaned by washing with a sponge mop (don't flood the floor — it can loosen the seams), then drying thoroughly. If you wish to wax, use a wax especially designed for vinyl. Most vinyl floors have an excellent gleam without waxing.

See the chart at the end of this chapter for information on measuring floors before buying resilient flooring.

CERAMIC TILE

Ceramic tile — tile made of baked clay — has been used for home decorating since the time of the Romans and probably before. A few years ago it was found mainly in bathrooms in rather dull, albeit practical, designs. It is now moving into more areas of the home in an almost endless variety of color and design.

Glazed ceramic tile is more likely to wear well and is easier to keep clean than unglazed tile. Unglazed tile must be waxed to keep dirt from entering its surface; glazed tile can be cleaned by mopping.

Tile is cold to the touch, making it excellent for use in areas which are warm throughout the year. It can be used for many decorative purposes, from floors to windowsills (where it forms a protective barrier against, for instance, drips from plants) to fireplace walls, in imitation of old European homes.

Ceramic tile is expensive but depending on other furnishings can give a home a formal or informal touch as few floor coverings can. Never wax glazed ceramic tile — it's slippery enough without it.

TERRAZZO

Terrazzo is made of marble chips mixed with cement; these floors are popular in some apartment houses. They were originally limited to porches but may be found in any room now.

Terrazzo is one of the least comfortable floors to stand on for any length of time. For that reason, rugs or carpets are recommended for any room except perhaps a short hallway or a room where people will be almost always sitting down.

Terrazzo floors have a finish which is put on when they are made. Washing should be done carefully to avoid streaking the floor with dirty water. Wash with a sponge mop; dry immediately. If streaking results, go over the floor in the same way with water containing a water softener.

MARBLE

Marble floors are found mainly in public buildings such as museums, although a few homes have some marble flooring. Sometimes marble tops furniture and, if you are living in a very old house, you may have a marble fireplace.

Marble is extremely soft, and has a tendency to pit. It also stains easily. Occasionally, because it is so soft and porous, a stain which is left alone will work its way out the other side.

Marble should be vacuumed with the dusting attachment of a tank-type vacuum cleaner, washed when necessary with water and water softener (hard water can coat the marble with a film), and waxed with a wax suitable for marble.

Stains are extremely difficult to remove from marble once they have set. Undiluted chlorine bleach covered with a pad or sponge and left for several hours may work.

MIRRORS

Mirrors are usually considered accessories to a room, but mirror material can form part of a room's background, too. At one time, mirrored floors were used in homes; this proved not only impractical (the mirrors tended to break) but also somewhat unnerving to visitors. Mirrored ceilings require both a special personality in their owners and special installation. Leave the installation to a professional.

Mirrored walls, however, are becoming more and more popular. Mirror can either be bought in large sheets or, much less expensively, in mirror tiles. These tiles do not reflect entirely correctly but they do expand a room if used in large enough numbers.

Mirror tiles can go on the wall, above a fireplace, all over one side of a narrow hallway to make it look larger, on a windowsill to protect the sill from water from plants and to reflect the sky, and on the back of doors to provide full-length mirrors for dressing.

Mirror is cleaned in the same way as any glass. One of the spray-on window cleaners, wiped off with paper towels, is the easiest way of cleaning mirror.

The charts which follow tell how to determine the square footage of your room for paint or wallpaper purchase, figuring square footage for floor covering purchase, and describe the characteristics of various carpet fibers and carpet types.

FORMULA FOR FIGURING AMOUNT OF WALL PAINT NEEDED

Length around room in feet *times* height from baseboard to ceiling in feet *equals* total square feet *minus* 20 square feet for every three openings (doors, windows, fireplaces) *divided by* 450 square feet *equals* gallons of paint required. (Average gallon of paint covers 500 square feet; 450 is being used here for safety.)

FORMULA FOR FIGURING AMOUNT OF WALLPAPER NEEDED

Length around room in feet *times* height from baseboard to ceiling in feet *equals* total square feet *minus* 20 square feet for every three openings (doors, windows, fireplaces) *divided by* 30 square feet *equals* number of rolls of wallpaper needed. (Although there are 35 square feet in every roll of wallpaper, 30 square feet is used here for safety.)

FORMULA FOR FIGURING AMOUNT OF FLOOR COVERING NEEDED

Length of room in feet (measure around walls) *times* width of room in feet (measure around walls) *plus* length times width of any alcoves in room *equals* total number of square feet of floor space. Then use one of these formulas:

For rugs and carpets: total divided by 9 equals square yardage needed.

For resilient flooring: 12″ tiles — buy same number as you have square feet.
9″ — *multiply* number of square feet by 144 (square inches) and *divide* by 81 (square inches of tile) for number of tiles.

For paint: total divided by 450 equals number of gallons needed.

FLOOR COVERINGS, RUGS, AND CARPETS

Name	Description
Acrylic	Resilient; dyes well; soils easily but cleans easily
Asphalt tile	Inexpensive; quiet; easily damaged, subject to cracks; hard to find
Cotton	Soft; easily cleaned; tends to mat; not widely available
Cushioned vinyl	More comfortable to stand on than other vinyls (see vinyl)
Homogenous vinyl	Vinyl throughout; custom designs possible
Inlaid vinyl	Pattern goes through vinyl completely; no chance of wearing off as with roto vinyl
Linoleum	Resists grease, not alkaline substances; inexpensive; may be hard to find
Nylon	Resilient; abrasion resistant; cleans easily
Olefin	Stain resistant, cleans easily; inexpensive; crushes easily
Polyester	Soft; dirt resistant; may pill and shed
Rayon	Inexpensive; crushes easily; wears least well of coverings
Roto vinyl	Inexpensive; pattern may wear off
Vinyl	Generally sturdy; easily cleaned
Vinyl-asbestos	Moderately priced; easy to clean

13

Planning Your Lighting

The light you use in your home can make a tremendous difference in how you feel about that home, how your eyes feel, and how comfortable you are when entertaining. Our eyes are so adaptable that we may not notice that the light in our homes is insufficient. For instance, we may not enjoy cooking, but not realize that this is because the overhead light in the kitchen causes the cabinets to cast a shadow on our work space.

TYPES OF LIGHTING

There are two main types of electric light available for home use—fluorescent and incandescent. Both have advantages and disadvantages. Both are better for some locations than for other locations. Take these considerations into account in doing your planning.

Fluorescent fixtures and lamps are made so that, unlike incandescent bulbs, once you've chosen your wattage you're stuck with it. The size of the fixture determines the wattage. You can't replace a low wattage tube with a higher or a higher with a lower.

173

Fluorescent tubes last longer than incandescent bulbs (an advantage for hard-to-reach places) and generate less heat (an advantage in enclosed areas, say, book shelves).

Fluorescent tubes also use less energy than do incandescent lights. This is one reason they are used in many public buildings. On the other hand, fluorescent tubes tend to give a somewhat cold light and, since fluorescents, in creating light, flash on and off at an extremely high speed, they can be very tiring to the eyes.

Incandescent bulbs don't last as long as fluorescent tubes, but each bulb is less expensive for its light than each fluorescent. Most people consider incandescent light more like daylight than fluorescent light is, but actually incandescent light is redder than daylight.

WATTAGES

Both fluorescent tubes and incandescent bulbs come in various wattages and colors. The watt is a measurement of electric consumption, not the amount of light given. However, both fluorescent and incandescent bulbs are sold by wattage. The brightness of a fluorescent tube of 40 watts is about equal to that of a 100-watt incandescent.

Wattage gives you a rough indication of the amount of light you will receive, but the important figure is the number of lumens, which measures actual light given. Recently, manufacturers have begun to provide figures for both lumens and expected hours of life on incandescent bulb packages. It is worthwhile to compare these figures among brands.

FLUORESCENT LIGHTING

Channels and tubes for fluorescent lights are most widely available in 20 watts, 30 watts, and 40 watts. The length of the tube determines the wattage. The longer the tube, the higher the wattage. Usually, 20-watt tubes are 24 inches long, 30-watt tubes are 36 inches long, and 40-watt tubes are 48 inches long.

The best fluorescent lighting for home use is "color-improved" in either deluxe warm white or deluxe cool white. The deluxe warm white is closest to the incandescent lighting most people prefer. If you cannot find deluxe warm white, warm white is usually preferable to cool white for homes.

Fluorescent lights are also available in various other types, including plant growth tubes. These are special tubes designed to mimic daylight and encourage plants to grow.

INCANDESCENT BULBS

Incandescent bulbs are available in greater variety than fluorescent tubes. A dimmer (also called a rheostat) can be used to control incandescent lighting in a room from a wall switch. You can have the lighting at its brightest or lower it for softer lighting. As yet, this is not possible with fluorescent lights, although a dimmer for use with fluorescent light is in the process of development.

Incandescent bulbs come in very frosted, somewhat frosted, and clear form. Manufacturers have different names for these bulbs. Look at the various types on display when you shop to see which is which.

Use the somewhat frosted bulb for most purposes unless you really like paying for light you don't get. If they are too bright, buy a lower wattage rather than a more heavily frosted bulb. Any bulb which is enclosed entirely, as in a ceiling fixture, so that the bulb itself doesn't show at all, should have a completely clear bulb. Unfortunately, these are often hard to find.

Since bulbs tend to burn out more or less on schedule, replace all bulbs in a ceiling fixture when the first one goes. The bulbs that are not yet burned out can be used for lamps that are easier to change.

OTHER INCANDESCENT TYPES

Among the many different types of incandescents are tubes which can be used, for instance, under kitchen counters. High-intensity bulbs are small bulbs which give a very clear, bright light. They need special lamps or fixtures.

Incandescent bulbs come in various tints and colors which cast a different light from the usual incandescent bulb. Pink and yellow are the most widely available. Many people like to use a rose bulb in a lamp for a special effect. If you plan to use colored bulbs, buy one and test it in the various rooms in your home. Certain pigments used in dyes and paints react differently to these colors.

Long-life bulbs are another form of incandescent. They tend to last about three times as long as others. They are good for hard-to-reach places, but are more expensive and give less light for the same amount of energy than other bulbs.

And consider a few other points.

• You may want a light in a closet. You can get a battery-operated light for this purpose which goes on automatically when the door opens, off when it closes.

• Lights outside the front and back doors of your home are both useful and welcoming to guests. It helps, too, if a light shines on your house number.

• Timers are a good idea if you are out a lot but want your home to look as if you're in. You can use timers to turn a light on at dusk, for instance. Timers are used to turn electricity on and off. Plug the device you want turned on into the timer. A timer can turn on a radio or an electric coffee pot as well as your living room lamps.

• To figure what you need in the way of lighting, plan on one watt of incandescent light for each square foot of floor space. If your walls are dark or your ceiling is high, make it three watts per square foot. High-ceilinged rooms and rooms with dark walls need more lighting than other rooms because there is less reflected light from walls and ceilings in them.

ACCENT AND BACKGROUND LIGHTING

Two types of lighting are used in the home. Background, or general, lighting should be soft light by which we can see for conversation but not for working. Accent lighting is lighting for a special area — to highlight a dining table, for instance — or purpose — to work by, for example.

In theory, background lighting comes from fixtures in the ceiling and lights in the cornices over draperies, while accent lighting usually comes from lamps or low-hanging fixtures. Lamps, however, quite often fill both needs.

Lamps are both decorative and a source of light. The shades should be such that the bulb is completely hidden. If it isn't, try to get a longer or shorter harp (the part that supports the shade) to raise or lower the shade. Translucent shades provide the most light.

Floor lamps are popular, as they can be moved from place to place; table lamps are almost always used on end tables.

RECESSED LIGHTING

Down light

Eyeball light

Desk lamps are essential for people working or studying. Light should come from your right if you are left-handed, from your left if you are right-handed.

Hanging fixtures have come back into fashion after being out for some time. They can be used to define a section of a room — a dining area, for instance — and they come in many styles. Be sure any hanging fixture is big enough to supply sufficient light and in a position where heads will not bump into it.

Recessed lighting is usually found in the ceiling. There must be about a foot between the ceiling and the floor above to install it. It can be used for background lighting, with a series of lights pointing to the floor, or to highlight an object with a spotlight. Fluorescent lighting can be put behind a translucent false ceiling. The coolness of fluorescent lights in burning makes them safe to use in such an enclosed space.

PLANNING LIGHTING

Lamp	Height	Shade	Incandescent Wattage
Table	About 40″ from floor to bottom of shade	About 16″ wide at bottom; must cover bulb	About 200 in any combination (such as one 3-way 200; two bulbs of 100 watts each; three 75-watt bulbs)
Desk or study	About 15″ from table or desk to bottom of shade	If high intensity, supplement with general light	At least 200 in any combination
Floor	At least 48″ from floor to bottom of shade	As for table lamp	300 watts preferred in any combination for reading, card playing; for other purposes, at least 200 in any combination

14

Finishing Touches: Fireplaces, Plants, Accessories

Throughout this book we've been stressing ways to bring your own personality into your home. Attention to detail in many areas creates the very special look of individuality that good decorating seeks. You probably won't be able to — and won't want to — finish every final detail of your home. This aspect of decorating is one which grows and changes over time as it should, expressing the changing interests of you and your family.

What are some of these details? They can include your front hall closet (think about wallpapering or painting it in a color that works with the rest of the house, using matching hangers), the pictures you hang on the walls (and be sure to leave room for children's drawings, photographs), or the color schemes of the paper napkins you use. Fireplaces, plants, and various accessories are among the features which help give a home warmth and personality. This chapter discusses them with, at the end, a quick overview of methods for hanging items from walls.

FIREPLACES

Fireplaces are traditional, romantic, and often a decorative feature of a room. They can provide heat (although not really efficiently) and a built-in accent.

Not all fireplaces are attractive by today's standards, and not all fireplaces are working fireplaces. If you have a home with a fake fireplace and an ugly mantel, consider having it taken out altogether so the space can be used for something else. If this seems too expensive or too drastic, or you like the look of the fireplace, you can purchase a fake fire. These use electric lights and are not very realistic. Failing that, you can fill the fireplace with either a fireplace fan (not terribly expensive) or plants. Plants are one of the most attractive solutions, but the plants themselves will have to be changed frequently — they won't get enough light to live.

The working fireplace doesn't, of course, present the same problems as the non-working fireplace. There is something very attractive about flickering flames and the warmth of a fire in the fireplace, making a natural center for a room.

Although fireplaces are not considered the most efficient source of heat (a great deal of the warmth escapes up the chimney with the smoke), they can be used to replace or supplement your heating system. Charcoal, although relatively expensive as a fireplace fuel, burns efficiently and emits very little pollution. Never light a fire in the fireplace without opening a window, no matter how cold it may be. All fires use up oxygen in the air as they burn. Human beings need oxygen to live. If there is not sufficient fresh air entering a room where a fire is burning in a fireplace, the people in the room will become unconscious and eventually die.

If your home does not have a working fireplace and you would like one, investigate various possibilities such as a Franklin stove. All fireplaces must be properly vented (have a way for smoke and gases, such as carbon monoxide, to be carried away) and this should be done by a professional in fireplace installation.

Fireplaces have their own accessories.

• A *fireplace screen* is essential. This keeps sparks from flying out of the fireplace and onto the carpet and helps keep you and your family from getting too close to the fire. Screens

FIREPLACE ACCESSORIES

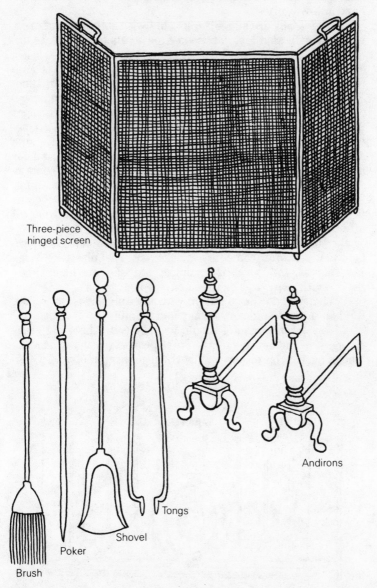

Three-piece
hinged screen

Brush

Poker

Shovel

Tongs

Andirons

are usually fairly expensive new but are often available second-hand at lower prices.

• *Andirons* are supports, usually with some kind of decoration, which hold logs for wood fires so air can circulate underneath. They come in many reproductions of antique styles; early American andirons are especially popular. Brass andirons are handsome but have to be polished now and then. Wrought iron andirons are more practical, but less formal.

• *Fireplace tools* are something else you may want to get if you have a fireplace. They are not essential but are attractive and useful. They usually hang on a stand and consist of a shovel, a brush, a poker, and a pair of large tongs, all for moving the fire around once it's burning. These, too, come in various metals, including brass. Brass requires polishing. There are lacquers available for coating brass items such as fire tools, but unfortunately they have a tendency to wear off after a time, leaving a somewhat uneven surface.

• Most fireplaces have a mantel over them. This is where typical accessories come in — clocks, large candlesticks, large jars, plants, and the classic painting of a ship on the chimney breast with a spyglass on the mantelpiece.

What you decide to put on your mantelpiece is up to you, but here are a few ideas you may find helpful.

Items on the mantel should be balanced. Three big vases on one side and nothing on the other probably won't work. The balancing can be either symmetrical or asymmetrical. Sym-

MANTEL

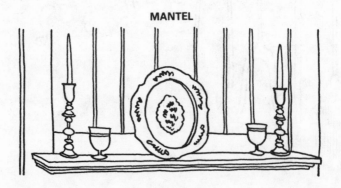

MANTEL

metrical balance occurs when, for instance, there are identical objects at each side and, perhaps, a clock in the middle. Asymmetrical balance is achieved by unlike objects which give the impression of having the same total weight. A very large vase of flowers, for instance, might be balanced by a grouping of small cups from a collection.

PLANTS

The role of plants in people's homes and lives ranges from accessory to career. You can best judge for yourself how you feel about your plants.

If you plan to use your plants solely as accessories, you may need to replace them often, as the places where they look most attractive may not be the healthiest for them. If your plants are a way of life for you, you will need specialized plant information and may want to consider such things as glass shelves built across your windows to hold plants.

Here are some hints on using plants as accessories.

• Plants grown for their foliage are usually more attractive for a longer time than are plants grown for their flowers. Among the easiest plants to grow indoors and use as accessories are the several types of philodendron. They tolerate dim light without getting too upset.

• Plant lights can be used to supplement or replace sunlight to a certain extent. Such lights can be either fluorescent or incandescent and are designed especially for use with plants. Ordinary artificial light, both fluorescent and incandescent, can also help plants grow. If you have a plant you want to keep in the living room on an end table all the time, you may find it can manage if you leave the lamp on the table on for about eight hours.

DRIED AND ARTIFICIAL FLOWERS

If you like plants as accessories but feel you can't spend the time needed to care for them, or if you are convinced that you will never have a green thumb, consider some alternatives.

• Inexpensive dried flowers and leaves (everlastings) can be bought in many flower shops and arranged in big bouquets. Mix the flowers you use and be prepared to discard these cheap flowers when they become too dusty. Some large stores and specialty shops offer extremely elegant packages of everlasting flowers. These are expensive but you may feel they are worth it as a one-time investment. Dust these flowers with the dusting tool of your tank-type vacuum cleaner; if you can regulate the suction, put it on low suction to avoid taking the flowers into the vacuum with the dust.

• Fabric flowers can be extremely attractive, but they range in appearance from good to terrible. They can be bought in most department stores. Shop around. Generally, the most expensive are the most attractive. These, too, should be used in large quantities to make an effect. They can be mixed with everlastings.

• China flowers, fruits, and vegetables and those made of other very hard substances such as alabaster cannot be considered to resemble real ones in the way fabric ones do, but they are attractive. These are most commonly used for table centerpieces but can be used anywhere.

• Plastic flowers, fruits, and plants are much less successful. This may be because while the china ones are obviously false the plastic are just not quite real enough. Plastic plants, of course, are much loved by office building decorators, which may be another reason they don't look quite right in homes. If you feel you must use them, use them very sparingly and try to mix in some real flowers or leaves, too. And do wash the leaves regularly.

MIRRORS

Mirrors are decorative, room expanding, and functional. Ideally, there should be a full-length mirror on the back or front of at least one door in every room where people will be dressing. There should also be one near the front door so people can make a last-minute check before leaving home.

Don't pay for a full-length one-piece mirror that is not plate glass. Other glass will distort reflections. If you find the plate glass is too expensive, don't buy a cheap full-length mirror. You'll save money by buying mirror tiles, and the design of the tiles somehow offsets the disadvantage of the distortion.

Try to place mirrors where they will reflect an attractive image. This is not always possible but is desirable.

Mirrors with frames pose a double problem. Choose a frame you like which fits your room and the mood you are trying to create, but also be sure the mirror does a good job of reflecting.

PICTURES

Pictures are another popular home accessory. They can range from an ancestral portrait to a painting by an unknown contemporary artist. Unless you are a millionaire and know a great deal about art, don't buy paintings as an investment. There are too many frauds and near-frauds being perpetrated today by companies selling more or less mass-produced paintings. To make these paintings, the artist will line up fifty canvases and then paint, say, fifty trees on them, add fifty mountains, throw in fifty cows, and, finally, add one detail which is slightly changed on each painting. There's nothing wrong with buying a mass-produced painting if you really like it. Just don't fool yourself into thinking it's an investment that will increase in value.

Prints are fine. Many experts feel they would rather have a print of a painting by a great artist than an original painting by an inferior artist. Again, select the print by what you like rather than by what you think you should like.

It is much less expensive to frame pictures yourself than to have them professionally framed. You can buy frames inexpensively in many places. Ten-cent stores often have quite nice plain wooden frames complete with mats and glass. Department stores often offer metal and clear acrylic plastic frames.

If you buy a picture or print already framed, remember that you are paying a substantial price for the frame. Be sure you like it.

You may not want a frame at all for some of the pictures you plan to hang on your wall. If you have a poster, for instance, find out from a stationery store, an art supply store, a photostat maker, or a framer if you can have it mounted on stiff cardboard and covered with some kind of protective coating. Maps make very effective wall decorations of this type, too.

GROUPED PICTURES

If you have many small pictures and want to tell a big story on one wall, group them together. It doesn't matter if they are different sizes. Plot on paper how you want the finished display to look. Most experts feel that a group of pictures looks best if at least one horizontal edge of one picture and one vertical edge of another are even with each other.

Most pictures are hung at what is eye level when people are standing. Be sure this is what you want. In a living room,

GROUPED PICTURES

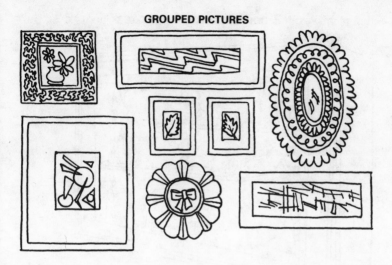

for instance, where people are most likely to be sitting, it seems foolish to hang pictures so high they can only be admired when people are standing.

ASHTRAYS

Whether or not you smoke yourself, ashtrays are something to include in your accessories. If you don't smoke, you may hope to discourage smoking by not displaying ashtrays. In that case, have them nearby. You can whip them out when someone who smokes lights up. Many smokers are thoughtless and may smoke in your home whether you want them to or not. With the ashtrays, they're less likely to damage your furniture.

If you like ashtrays displayed, perhaps because you're a smoker yourself, choose them for three features — safety, size, and appearance.

There are many fireproof plastic ashtrays on the market now, but they tend to become marked by burning cigarettes. Glass, china, and ceramic ashtrays stay attractive longer.

Ashtrays should be large but not too large. Too large ashtrays encourage people to fill them too full.

COLLECTION DISPLAY BOXES

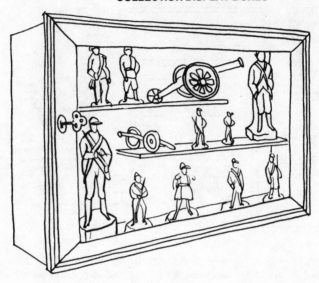

Ashtrays designed so that cigarettes fall into a bottom compartment are good in theory but not always in practice. Quite often the cigarette going into the bottom is still lit and sets the other cigarettes on fire.

Indentations on ashtrays to hold cigarettes look like a good idea but are actually somewhat dangerous. A cigarette can be forgotten and fall off to burn something else.

Unusual ashtrays can be quite attractive. Both ceramic cereal bowls and old-fashioned ceramic soap dishes make good ashtrays.

COLLECTIONS

Collections can be effective accessories, too. They're often overlooked as decorative items, however.

A few items from a collection make a nice accent on a coffee or end table or on a small shelf in the hall. A large collection deserves a good display. Consider one of the collection display cases available from hobby shops. These are boxes which can be hung on the wall or stood on another piece of furniture. They have many small compartments and the front is covered with glass.

Very large collections need a good deal of space. A bookcase can be used for such things as miniature furniture, the top of a secretary or china cabinet for china, and the wall of a hallway for old family pictures.

Collections are fine on mantelpieces, too. In that case, the prime consideration should be the best display for the collection rather than concern about balance and so forth.

Collections bring us to our last point. Accessories are a way of bringing warmth into your house and this warmth should be sincere. Leave room in your decorating plans for the whale your child made in woodworking class, your grandmother's thimble, and things you'll acquire as life goes on.

HANGING THINGS ON WALLS

Many of the things we've mentioned here may require fastening to a wall. Here is what to do to avoid having the things fall off again. Remember that most methods of hanging involve some permanent damage to the wall.

Picture hooks are probably the best-known method of hanging pictures and mirrors on walls. They can be bought in many places, including hardware stores, ten-cent stores, and home centers. There is an indication of how much weight each hook will hold on the package. This assumes, of course, that the wall itself is not crumbling into dust.

HANGING DEVICES

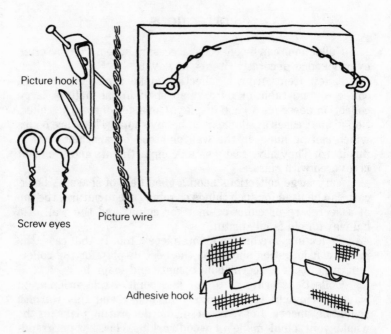

Picture hook

Screw eyes

Picture wire

Adhesive hook

Picture hooks rely on a nail which is hammered into the wall at an angle and holds the hook. Picture wire is placed on the back of the mirror or picture by fastening it to screw eyes (circular pieces of metal with a screw tip) fastened to the frame. Two picture hooks make a picture less likely to tip unevenly. You will have to figure carefully how much wire to use as it is drawn taut by these two hooks.

Moisture-activated adhesives can be used for hanging things on walls. There are fabric-backed picture hooks designed for use when the wall is not right for taking a nail. These are used in pairs — one on the wall, one on the picture or mirror. They hook over each other.

Some plastic hooks for holding rings or towels come with a thick adhesive on the back. This is moistened, then rubbed until it is a thick liquid. The hook is then pressed to the wall and held until a bond is formed.

There are also paper-backed spongy squares which have glue on both sides. The paper is removed and the squares are stuck onto the object to be hung and then to the wall. They are good for mirror tiles and other very lightweight things. You can use several on one object for added strength.

Full-length mirrors usually come with their own fasteners to hang them to doors. These are usually clear plastic clips. The clips are screwed to the door, the mirror is slid under the edge of the clips, and the screws are tightened so that the clips hold the mirror firmly.

Very heavy things — large oil paintings, framed mirrors, hanging cabinets — need more elaborate installations to hang on walls. Use toggle anchors or bolts on plastered hollow walls. These have a piece which is pushed through the wall to the back. It opens and hugs the back of the wall. Concrete walls should have plastic anchor screws, as should brick walls. The plastic anchor is driven into the wall through a hole and the screw is screwed into that.

For best support of hanging cabinets, brackets for bookshelves, and so forth, drive the plastic anchor into a stud in the wall. A stud is a wood beam perpendicular to the floor. These beams are supposed to be spaced sixteen inches apart. Sometimes they are. To find a stud, you can use something called a stud finder (a type of magnet which locates the nails in the stud), you can tap the wall (the wall will sound hollow, the stud solid), or you can look along the baseboard for the nails which should show where the baseboard has been nailed to the studs.

Drill the holes for the anchors and screws with an electric drill, using a suitable size drill bit. For drilling into brick or concrete, you will need a carbide drill bit.

15

Certain Rooms Need Extra Thought

Because there is a trend in decorating toward multiple-use rooms, rooms that are used for more than one purpose and that have more in common in the way they are decorated than they have differences, this book is not divided into sections on specific rooms. Nevertheless, there are certain rooms which do require a little extra thought because they are used in special ways. These rooms are the bathroom, the kitchen, the children's room, and the family room.

REQUIREMENTS

What do these different rooms have in common?

They all must be easy to clean — kitchens and bathrooms for sanitary reasons, children's and family rooms so that they can be enjoyed freely.

They should have hard-wearing furniture. Fragile furniture doesn't belong in any of these rooms. And they should be both efficient and comfortable.

The floor should be easy to clean, but in rooms where people will sit on the floor, comfort is at least equally important.

Here are some suggestions.

• For the kitchen and bath, one of the resilient floor coverings or (for the bath) ceramic tile work well.

• For the children's room and the family room, a resilient floor covering or a wood floor, topped by several small nylon fluffy soft rugs. These can be found in bath shops if not in rug departments. These rugs should be small enough to be washed in the machine. If you buy one extra, you can always have one in the wash being cleaned and others on the floor. They should have a non-skid backing.

STORAGE

Storage is essential in these rooms. Children's rooms need adequate storage for toys. Toy shelves seem to work better than toy chests, although chests are all right if necessary. The objection to chests is that it's hard to find a particular toy in a chest, and children tend to dump all the toys on the floor to find one.

• Kitchens need cupboards, drawers, and hooks of some kind to hold cooking utensils, cooking supplies, and tableware.

• Bathrooms need storage space for shampoo, soap, toilet paper, toothpaste, toothbrushes, shaving gear, drugs, and so forth.

• The family room should have storage space for both board and large games and for the many projects that will be going on there, from painting to railroad train running. Space for extra card tables and folding chairs is also desirable.

• Additional storage can often be found in one of these rooms by enclosing sinks. If you are panelling a family room, consider bringing the panelling out far enough from the wall to provide storage space.

Don't overlook the walls for storage space. Invest in hanging wall cabinets, shelves on brackets. See the accessories section for details on how to hang things on walls.

FURNITURE

The furniture in these rooms must be the kind that can take hard usage. Vinyl upholstery, synthetic plastic table and cabinet tops, and enamel-painted furniture can all be scrubbed if necessary.

• The wall covering should be either scrubbable or a paint which can be renewed as often as possible. If you don't want your children to write or to post things on the walls of their rooms or the family room, put up something such as stick-on cork in an area at least six feet by six feet and let them do what they want with it.

• In children's rooms, family rooms, and kitchens, it's valuable to have some space for a table or desk for studying, working, or planning. This table can do double duty for meals or snacks.

• Curtains or draperies should be informal and fun. Machine-washable permanent press café curtains are ideal. For kitchens, café curtains avoid the danger of fire from a long curtain being set alight by the stove. In all rooms, it's an advantage to have curtains that can be easily cleaned and rehung.

16

Saving Energy

Energy saving has become a serious consideration for everyone as we've watched the price of all kinds of energy go up, up, and away out of sight. In this section we will discuss the relatively easy things you can do to save energy in ventilating and lighting your home.

There are three major ways to save energy in the home. One is by saving on heat, one is by saving on air conditioning, and the third is by saving on lighting.

VENTILATION

To save on heat, begin by checking windows and doors which lead to the outside. This is where a tremendous amount of heat (and, in the summer, coolness) is lost.

Start by caulking the outside of the windows and doors, applying weather stripping to the inside. Caulk and weather stripping can be found in hardware stores and home centers; the instructions on the packages are usually quite good.

Even if you have double-paned windows, consider adding storm windows if you live in a very cold area. A storm window is a second window placed outside the regular window which effectively seals off the edges so cold air cannot seep either in or out. Unless your winters are extremely cold, you probably will not find it worth adding storm windows to double-paned windows that are less than fifteen square feet in area.

Storm doors are less important than storm windows for most homes. However, if you do not already own a screen door, get a storm door which is made so that a section slides out to be replaced with a screen section in the summer. A dual-duty door is worth the investment. If you already have a screen door, you will not save enough on energy to make it worthwhile to buy a storm door.

Shades, draperies, and curtains all help keep cold air from coming in or going out of the house. They help a little when they are open by adding to the effectiveness of the weather stripping, but they help a lot more when they are closed. On extremely hot or cold days, keep shades down and draperies closed.

The British use an additional item to keep cold air where they want it. They use long, round, thin, stuffed pieces of fabric, usually called sausages and occasionally made in the shape of a snake, as an extra air block at the bottom of doors. They work surprisingly well.

To make one of these, measure the bottom of the door and add about ten inches — two inches for a seam at each side and eight inches to be sure the snake can fit snugly against the door. Cut a strip of fabric this length by about twelve inches. Make a one-inch seam on the long side and one short end of the length of fabric, stitching with the right sides together. Turn the fabric right side out and stuff. Use batting (a material made for stuffing), rags, even old stockings or panty hose. Stitch the end closed. If you wish, you can cut one end in a diamond shape and embroider a snake's face on it.

Use exhaust fans rather than windows to ventilate places such as kitchens and bathrooms. The exhaust fan is both more efficient and less likely to interfere with the energy-saving measures you have taken.

Some people worry about the lack of ventilation in well-sealed homes. Don't. Most homes exchange between 70 percent and 100 percent of the air inside the house with the air outside the house hourly through walls and small openings. You only need to exchange 20 percent for health. It's unlikely that any of these measures will lower the air exchange in your home even to that extent.

LIGHTING

Conserving on the use of electric lighting is another way of saving energy. Although electric light does not consume as much current as, for instance, an electric iron (heat production by electricity requires a great deal of energy), the watts used for lighting do add up, especially as lights are usually on longer than more energy consuming appliances.

On the other hand, don't overdo energy conservation by turning off all lights. There is no reason to strain your eyes. Continue to use the wattage of bulbs and fluorescents you are used to, but don't waste lighting.

Keep most lights turned off when people aren't home, but leave a light or two on both to welcome you home and to deter burglars.

It costs a certain amount to turn a switch on or off. However, if you will be out of a room more than twenty minutes, even if the room is lit by fluorescents, the energy you save by turning off the light is worthwhile.

17

Getting What You Want

Unfortunately, even when you are armed with the knowledge we have compiled for this book, it may be difficult to get exactly what you want. You may have trouble finding what you want in a store because you don't know the special store language. Salespeople may tell you that the item isn't made at all, isn't made any more, or is just the same as something else.

Once you have chosen just what you want, there may be delivery delays. This chapter is designed to help you with these problems.

STORE LANGUAGE

Furniture, more than most other retail items, is referred to in specialized language with which most of us are unfamiliar. Here is a brief vocabulary. It includes the terminology of the largest stores with the most departments. Smaller stores have fewer divisions and are less likely to stick to them.

• *Bedding* covers mattresses, box springs, a few purely decorative headboards in most stores (brass headboards, for instance), and metal bed frames on casters. It often includes sofa beds and recliners.

- *Bedroom* is short for bedroom furniture. It means case goods almost exclusively — chests of drawers, night tables, wood bed frames. If you buy several pieces of one style, you will be buying a bedroom suite. Don't be surprised to hear this pronounced "suit."
- *Borax* is the furniture industry's term for junk furniture. If your salesperson tells you the furniture you are looking at is borax, it may be the truth.
- *Case goods* is the term used for most wood furniture. Originally it referred only to furniture made in a box (case) shape, often fitted with drawers, such as a chest. The term *case goods* is usually used to distinguish items from upholstered goods and bedding.
- *Contemporary* is considered a more up-to-date term for *modern*. There is an implication of better taste than the usual *modern* in the word *contemporary*, but this may not be justified.
- *Dining room* is short for dining room furniture and includes most dining tables, chairs, and side boards. Less expensive dining room furniture may find its way into a completely different department such as kitchen or dinette furniture, or may be on the same floor in "summer furniture."
- *Hard goods* is the term for all non-textile items in the average store. Hard goods sometimes includes white goods. White goods are refrigerators, washing machines, and stoves, so called because they used to be available only in white.
- *Living room* stands for living room furniture but is much less likely to be a section of its own than bedroom and dining room. It usually includes only case goods. If a store has an occasional furniture section, "living room" will probably not exist as a separate category.
- *Modern furniture* is more or less self explanatory. It is used to describe stripped-down case goods and upholstered goods. It is usually in a special section of its own.
- *Occasional furniture* includes wood furniture such as coffee and end tables and a limited number of chairs, usually of the open stock dining room type. Don't look for card tables here, though. They're usually sold on another floor in another department called "adult games."
- *Open stock* refers to items which the manufacturer intends to continue to produce almost indefinitely. Buying open

stock means in theory that you can buy a few items in a particular style at one time and come back in a year or five years and add additional pieces in that style.

• *Upholstered* refers to upholstered furniture. An all-wood chair such as a dining room chair, even though it has an upholstered seat, is usually considered either dining room or occasional rather than upholstered. *Upholstered* includes all kinds of sofas, love seats, and chairs. Sofa beds and recliners may be in this section or in bedding.

• *Sectional furniture* is upholstered furniture which comes in sections. You can more or less design your own sofa by choosing a right-armed chair and a left-armed chair and putting an armless chair in the middle.

• *Summer furniture* is any kind of furniture suitable for use outside or inside in a summery room. Most summer furniture is relatively inexpensive; check here if you find some dining room prices, for instance, too high. Summer furniture includes rattan and wicker.

• *Traditional furniture* is any furniture reflecting a style from the past such as eighteenth-century English or one of the French styles. This category is sometimes further divided, depending on the size of the store, into sections devoted to furniture from one manufacturer or from one period, such as early American.

You will have noticed that some of the groupings make little sense. This is because most department store furniture departments are divided up by buyers and assistant buyers. Each buyer is constantly looking to see how he can expand both his space on the floor and the number of things he can sell. Usually, when a manufacturer adds a different category of furniture to an existing line, the buyer who has bought from him first gets to have the new item in his section.

FINDING AN ITEM

We mentioned that salespeople can be a problem when you are looking for a specific item by telling you it is either no longer made or never was. This is not altogether the result of wickedness, but more the result of ignorance combined with a desire to seem knowledgeable. You, however, are armed.

How can you be sure you'll get what you really want?

• Try to avoid feeling that you must buy something the day you start looking for it. This leads to desperation and a willingness to compromise where, perhaps, you should not compromise.

• Shop around. Go to several different types of stores if you can.

Check mail order catalogues, not only from the large mail order firms but also from small firms specializing in one area of home furnishings.

• If you find an intelligent salesperson or store owner who is both enthusiastic and knowledgeable, you've found a treasure. This person can not only find you what you want but also advise you on new items you may not know exist.

• If stores tell you items don't exist, ask to see catalogues. There are excellent catalogues for furniture, hardware, lighting fixtures, light bulbs, and tubes. Ask if the store will order the item for you.

• Remember that you are the customer. You are paying the store to supply you with what you want. In a sense, every person who works in that store is dependent on you for income — without customers, the store would fail. In a sense, you are doing the store a favor by being knowledgeable and requiring it to serve you.

GETTING DELIVERY

Delivery — getting the home furnishings you've ordered after you've found and paid for them — is one of the biggest problems in the furniture industry and one of the biggest concerns of consumer organizations. This is also where a decorator can save you from misery. The decorator will nag everyone for the items you've bought.

You will usually be promised delivery in six weeks. To be realistic, you should add at least another eight weeks to that date.

Most explanations, excuses, and reasons for delay in furniture deliveries (and occasionally in rug deliveries) appear inadequate. One reason (not an excuse, however) for delays, more important in wood furniture than in upholstered furniture, is that manufacturers often don't want to start making a style until they have enough orders to make it worth their while to tool up.

Furniture is held in inventory at a store's warehouse only in limited quantities and held in inventory at the manufacturer's warehouse in equally limited quantities.

When a new style is introduced, usually in January or July, the floor samples (the furniture you see in the store) may be all the store owns and may be the floor samples from the manufacturer's showroom.

The desire to wait to have enough orders to make tooling up worthwhile is also the reason that furniture deliveries are slow when business itself is slow. The manufacturers are waiting for enough orders to "cut." Searching out brand names and leading stores is no solution to the problem of poor delivery.

There are a few, usually small, furniture stores which sell only "from stock." They won't show you anything they don't have on hand. They are worth patronizing if you can find what you want.

Don't, whatever you do, get rid of the furniture you are using until the new furniture is in the door and you have thoroughly inspected it. This is one way of ensuring against settling for flawed furniture out of desperation.

In some areas of the country, stores must notify you if your furniture or whatever is delayed past the date promised. You are then given the option of cancelling your order and getting your money back or continuing to wait. If you cancel, of course, you still don't have the furniture — and the store still has the use of your money while you wait if you don't cancel.

KNOCKED-DOWN DELIVERY

One aspect of furniture delivery which is often overlooked is the question of what the furniture will be like when you receive it.

Will you receive a sofa or desk put together the way it was on the floor of the store? Or will you get a flat box containing all the parts needed to put it together and poor assembly directions, if any? This is something to ask any furniture store — no matter how reputable — before buying.

Many times the largest, best-known stores deliver everything in pieces (called knocked-down or KD in the trade), while the smaller furniture store, especially one that does its own deliveries, will put things together for you. It's worth shopping for this service unless you enjoy this type of puzzle.

The furniture industry has begun trying to convince the consumer that knocked-down furniture is good. You may hear the term *easy-to-assemble* used instead of knocked down. This term may be justified in the case of kit furniture ordered by mail, where you would pay more in shipping if the furniture were assembled, but it isn't in the case of finished furniture from a conventional retailer.

When you buy, ask if the furniture is supposed to be delivered assembled and if it is get your salesperson to write down on your sales slip that it is. If it isn't, and you like it enough to put it together yourself, find out in advance if you need anything in the way of special tools.

HOW TO COMPLAIN

If you have a complaint — whether it is about delivery, damaged merchandise, or anything else — start with the store itself. It's worth telephoning the store and asking the name of the president so you can address the letter to the top person. Some store presidents believe in sending boxes of candy to all complainers, too, so you may get a snack, if not your furniture.

If this doesn't work, go after the manufacturer. If you don't know the name of the manufacturer, check your sales slip. Sometimes the name is noted there. Wood furniture often has the manufacturer's name burned or stamped into the bottom. If it doesn't, look for chalked-on numbers on the bottom. The first number is the store's code number for that manufacturer, the second is the manufacturer's style number. Call the furniture department and simply ask "Who is manufacturer number so-and-so?"

You may be able to find the address out by asking the store. If not, check New York City (most likely Manhattan) and High Point, North Carolina, telephone books. Most furniture manufacturers have offices in one or both those cities.

Allow about three weeks for each of these maneuvers.

Complain in writing, including your name and address. Date the letter and make a carbon. Give as much detail as you can. Don't send the original sales slip to anyone; send photocopies.

If these attempts don't work, go to your city's consumer affairs agency if there is one. These agencies are old hands at handling home furnishings complaints and usually have a special person at each store they work with all the time. If there is no city consumer affairs agency, try your county or state. You can also try the Better Business Bureau. Because this organization is paid by the people it polices and can only bring real pressure on members, it may not be as strong as a consumer agency. It has a good general reputation, however, in the area of settling home furnishings complaints.

There is one industry association in home furnishings (there is another in major appliances such as refrigerators) designed to handle consumer complaints. It is called the Furniture Industry Consumer Advisory Panel, but its main purpose is to give consumers the feeling their complaints have a fair hearing. This group is paid for by furniture manufacturers. You can only complain about furniture which has a tag on it saying FICAP. The tag tells how to get in touch with the group.

The carpet industry had a similar organization called Carpet and Rug Consumer Advisory Panel but this has been abandoned.

Industry associations only intervene after you have tried to settle things directly with the manufacturer and consider yourself still dissatisfied.

The very fact that there are all these organizations taking an interest in settling home furnishings complaints indicates that there are a lot of complaints.

The best way to obtain satisfaction is to persist — again, this is the kind of job a decorator can take off your hands. If the decorator wants to charge you for the time, however, think carefully before agreeing.

Don't ever feel that because you are taking up a lot of someone else's time at the store or at the manufacturer you must apologize. You have the right to receive within a reasonable period of time and in good condition exactly what you bought.

Dictionary

In this section are definitions of alphabetically arranged words relating to home decorating. Where the home decorating pronunciation is different from the pronunciation used in everyday speech, or where the word itself is unfamiliar, we provide pronunciation information. Most trade names are not included except when they are commonly — and incorrectly — used as substitutes for the generic term in the home decorating industry. For example, we include Lucite and Plexiglas (trade names for acrylic plastic).

A

acetate Man-made fiber made from cellulose. Often used for luxurious decorating fabrics, as it resembles silk, acetate may also be mixed with other fibers for sheen, color, or to lower cost. Acetate is destroyed by acetone, a component of nail polish removers and some perfumes. When dyed, color not highly resistant to sunlight and atmosphere.

acrylic plastic Transparent and therefore sometimes used in place of glass, it is available tinted or clear. Acrylic plastic easily scratches and then looks cloudy. Waxing will help delay this. Don't use abrasive cleansers on it, as they destroy the transparency. Avoid putting hot items such as pans on it. Acrylic plastic melts under flame and loses its shape in boiling water. Under its trade names, probably the best-known of the man-made plastics used for furniture and accessories. Trade names include Plexiglas (made by Rohm and Haas) and Lucite (made by DuPont).

action chair See *reclining chair* under *chair*.

adaptation See *reproduction*.

alcove A recess which is part of a larger room. A dining alcove is big enough for a small dining table and chairs. A sleeping alcove is large enough for a

205

bed. Alcoves on either side of a fireplace are usually only large enough to hold bookcases.

al fresco From the Italian for "in the open air." It is used in English to describe activities that take place outside (especially eating, as in "al fresco dining").

aluminum See under *metal*.

ambiance or **ambience** (*ahm*-bee-ans) French word meaning "environment" or "atmosphere," usually used in English in the sense of "atmosphere," as in, "The house has a cozy ambiance."

antique Although *antique* can mean anything old, it usually refers to an item which is both old and valuable. In the case of home furnishings, the United States Customs Service defines anything 100 years old or older as an antique. Antiques can be imported duty free.

apron Finishing piece of flat wood, occasionally carved and decorated, usually placed along the front edge of wood furniture.

arch Curved structure which may support a ceiling but, in current architecture, is more likely to be purely decorative. Arches are considered softer in appearance than squares and straight lines. Arches rounded on the sides but pointed at the top are characteristic of the Gothic period in architecture.

area rug See under *rugs and carpets*.

armchair See under *chair*.

armless chair See under *chair*; *sectional furniture*.

Art Deco (*deh*-ko) Term used to describe ornate architecture and decoration of the late 1920s and 1930s. It is characterized by the use of a great deal of glass and mirror. Many movie theater lobbies of that period are in the Art Deco style.

Art Nouveau (noo-*vo*) French for "new art." Early twentieth-century style, stressing non-geometric shapes taken from nature, such as flower forms.

B

bachelor's chest See under *chest*.

bamboo Giant tropical grass used for lightweight furniture since it is hollow in the center. Characteristic shape of bamboo is reinterpreted in other materials — in china, on fabric, and on wallpaper, for example.

Barcelona chair (bar-se-*lo*-nuh) See under *chair*.

baseboard See section on molding, chapter 12, "Room Backgrounds."

basket Baskets woven of rushes, cane, grasses, and so forth are among the oldest containers known. At the moment they are very important in decorating; huge straw trunk baskets are used as coffee and end tables, round baskets as wastebaskets or to hold magazines, and small ones as letter holders. In their natural color baskets are usually a yellow-beige, called straw color, although some baskets, woven from dark grasses, are almost black. They are often dyed or painted. Baskets are copied occasionally in pottery and other materials, including sterling silver. *Basket-shaped* usually refers to a shape with rounded bottom.

beam Long piece, formerly usually of wood, used to support a building. Today, most structural beams are more likely to be made from another material, such as steel. Depending on their location, the mood of the room, and current fashion opinion, exposed beams are either decorative assets or liabilities. An awkward beam is one which breaks up the ceiling of a room, is placed asymmetrically in a room, is a threat to tall people, or otherwise interferes with desirable appearance. Today, artificial beams of lightweight plastic are popular additions to walls and ceilings in homes where a more rustic look is desired.

bean bag chair See under *chair*.

bed Furniture for lying down and sleeping. The shape of a bed and its size are determined by the *bed frame*. This is often made of wood but can also be metal. Bed frames raise a bed from the floor and support the mattress or box spring and mattress. The side rails of bed frames are often adjustable. A *headboard* is a decorative end for the top of the bed; headboards are often sold without the rest of the frame. A *footboard* is a decorative end for the bottom of the bed; footboards are sold only as part of an entire bed frame. Among the most common kinds of beds are:

canopy Bed with a canopy, usually a four-poster. See *four-poster*; *canopy*.

cot Narrow single bed about 30″ wide.

crib Bed for a baby or child up to about the age of three. Cribs have barred sides which usually can be raised and lowered so the child will not fall out. The Consumer Products Safety Commission has established standards for the distance between each bar on the sides of a crib and for assuring that exposed edges are smooth and not sharp. Cribs with these features are now available.

divan Bed placed on a metal frame, without side rails or headboard or footboard. Divan beds are usually between 27″ and 48″ wide.

double See *full-size*.

folding Bed with metal frame, usually on legs and caster, designed so it can be folded in half and stored in a closet. Folding beds are usually between 27″ and 48″ wide.

four-poster Bed, almost always of wood, with four posts, one at each corner. Four-posters can either support a canopy or be left plain.

full-size Bed, usually for two people, measuring 53″ or 54″ wide.

single Bed for one person, narrower than a twin bed, usually about 33″ wide.

twin Beds, sold in pairs and designed to be used together, each measuring about 38″ wide.

queen-size Bed, usually for two people, measuring about 60″ wide.

king-size Bed, usually for two people, measuring about 76″ wide.

water bed Bed whose mattress is man-made plastic fabric filled with water or gelatin, usually with wooden frame.

bed hangings Term used to refer to such things as curtains on four-poster beds. Originally designed to provide additional warmth for sleeping in unheated homes, bed hangings were considered unsanitary (and probably often were) by the beginning of the twentieth century. Easier methods of cleaning and a revival of interest in old-fashioned looks have contributed to the return of bed hangings. They are especially practical in synthetic fabrics which can be washed and rehung without ironing.

bedroom Room for sleeping. See under *bed*, and chapter 3, "Start with What You Have."

bedside chest See *end table* under *table*.

bench A long seat of wood or stone. See also *settle*.

bevel Term almost always used with the word *edge*. A bevel edge is one which, rather than being at right angles to the surface, is sloped, or, occasionally, rounded. This is an especially desirable feature on frameless mirrors.

bibelot (*bee*-buh-lo) See *bric-a-brac*.

blanket chest See under *chest*.

blinds See *shades and blinds*.

bookcase Furniture designed to hold books on one or more shelves. The traditional bookcase is rectangular, made of wood, and preferably has a back so the shelves don't sway. There are many variations. Bookcases may have glass shelves for a light effect, glass doors to keep dust away from the books, or grilled doors. Bookcases may be incorporated into other pieces of furniture, including *secretaries*, which often have space for books in the top section; *desks*, which may have space for books in the lower part; *breakfronts*, which are larger than secretaries and usually made in two pieces, with space for books in the top section; *bookcase headboards*, headboards at the top of a bed which include space for books; and such pieces of occasional furniture as *drum tables*.

box spring Rectangular object containing springs to provide additional support and bounce for the mattress on a bed. A true box spring does contain springs. Today, foam "box springs" are available for use with foam mattresses. These serve mainly to raise the mattress, rather than adding much to the comfort of the mattress. See chapter 9, "Buying Bedding."

braided rug See *rag rug* under *rugs and carpets*.

brass See *hardware*; see also under *metal*. See also chapter 7, "Buying Today's New Furniture."

breakfront See *bookcase*.

bric-a-brac All those little things (and some big ones) that either clutter or add character to a room depending on your point of view. Other words for bric-a-brac are *bibelots*, *curios*, *doodads*, *knick-knacks*, and *whatnots*. *Whatnot* also refers to a set of shelves used for storing bric-a-brac. Bric-a-brac can include anything from a china figurine to a fan to an antique book used purely for decoration.

brick Clay, molded into a rectangle, occasionally glazed, and joined with mortar or concrete. Brick is usually thought of as being a reddish color, but it can be yellow or white as well. Bare brick, either left in its natural state or painted, is currently popular for interiors. Artificial three-dimensional bricks which can be pressed into non-brick walls to give the appearance of brick are available. In order to hang anything on brick, holes must be drilled with a carbide drill bit, and plastic anchor screws are recommended.

brides' box A wooden box of any size from about one foot square up; term is usually applied to boxes from the Pennsylvania Dutch section of the United States, which are usually painted and decorated. Brides' boxes were used by young women to save items for their future homes. They were often filled before the husband-to-be was even in sight. See also *hope chest* under *chest*.

bridge table See *card table* under *table*.

broadloom Any carpet which is woven on a loom nine, twelve, fifteen feet, or wider. The term is often used incorrectly to imply high quality. See also under *rugs and carpets*.

buffet (buf-*fay* [correct pronunciation]; *buf*-it [occasional industry pronunciation]).   Flat-topped chest of drawers or long table used for holding china, silverware, and anything else used in setting a table and serving meals. Some buffets with drawers have one drawer lined with silver cloth. A buffet supper is one where guests do not sit at the table but serve themselves from a buffet, sideboard, or table. See also *silver cloth*.

built-in Description of furniture which is part of the structure of a room, as in "built-in bookcase" or "built-in closet."

bulb See *light bulb*; chapter 13, "Planning Your Lighting."

bureau See under *chest*.

burl See under *knot*.

butcher block Carefully joined high-quality wood used by butchers to cut meat on. Originally used only in kitchens, butcher block has become popular because of its appearance and graining for all types of tables and other surfaces. The typical butcher block is made of many rectangular pieces of solid wood.

butler's tray table See under *table*.

butterfly chair See under *chair*.

buttermilk The liquid left after churning butter from cream, used by early American settlers as a paint and paint additive. Certain paints made of modern materials attempt to imitate the faintly green color of new items painted with 100 percent buttermilk.

C

cabinet A case with drawers or shelves, usually closed by doors. Kitchen cabinets hold china, glassware, and food supplies, and may be made of metal (usually painted), wood, or a synthetic plastic. A *china cabinet* usually has glass doors and is designed to display a collection of china. *Record cabinets* are designed to hold phonograph records upright.

café curtains See under *curtains and draperies*.

campaign furniture Furniture designed to resemble that carried on military campaigns in the nineteenth century. It has extremely straight lines, usually accented with strips of metal, and much of it looks like luggage.

candelabra The plural of *candelabrum*, a large, branched holder for candles. *Candelabra* is occasionally used to describe electric lamps when the bulbs and bulb fixtures resemble candles.

candlestand See under *table*.

candlestick Anything which holds and supports a candle. Most candlesticks are made of metal, glass, or ceramic materials. When a candlestick is designed to hold more than one candle, it is usually called a candelabrum. See also *girandole*.

cane The hollow stem of certain giant reeds and grasses as well as the solid stem of palms, such as rattan. In furniture it appears as an open but firm woven surface and, as a decorative accent, is often used for the seats and backs of chairs.

canopy Any suspended covering. A canopy bed has a frame which is covered with fabric. The fabric is usually referred to as the canopy. Another term for canopy is *tester*.

card table See under *table*.

carpenter's rule A carpenter's rule, also known as a folding rule, is a measuring device, usually of wood, which is hinged so it can be carried compactly. Carpenter's rules are recommended for measuring distances over four feet as their stiffness gives greater accuracy than tape measures.

carpet See *rugs and carpets*.

carpet cushion See *padding*.

carpet pad See *padding*.

cart See *serving cart*.

case goods Furniture industry term describing most wood furniture that is not upholstery and bedding. Originally it referred only to furniture made in a box (case) shape, often fitted with drawers.

casters Small round wheels fastened to the bottom of furniture legs to permit furniture to be moved easily. Some casters can be locked in a non-rolling position.

casual furniture See *summer furniture*.

cedar chest See under *chest*.

centerpiece Decoration placed in the center of a dining table. Centerpieces are often flowers, but can be figurines, bowls of fruit, or anything else. Centerpieces should be low enough so that diners on opposite sides of the table can see each other for conversation.

chair Piece of furniture with a seat, legs, back, and, often, arms designed to seat one person. Following is a list of some of the more common types of chairs.

    armchair Chair with side pieces to support the sitter's arms. These side pieces are also called arms.

    armless chair Upholstered chair without arms. See also *sectional furniture*; *side chair*.

    Barcelona chair Chair made of curved chromed steel, with leather cushions. Originally designed by Mies van der Rohe for the German pavilion at the Barcelona World's Fair in 1929, this chair is a classic of modern design.

    bean bag chair Chair made of soft upholstery fabric (often vinyl) without any frame, often in a square shape, and filled with solid chips. The chair has no legs, and the chips move when the chair is sat in.

    bridge chair See *folding chair*.

    butterfly chair Chair made of bent metal (often wrought iron) in roughly the shape of a butterfly. The chair seat is a separate piece which hangs, somewhat in the manner of a hammock, from the metal. Also called a *sling chair*.

    chaise longue *(shez long* [correct pronunciation]; chayz lownj [occasional, incorrect, pronunciation]) French for "long chair." A chaise longue is a chair extended so that the seat is long enough to support the legs and feet. The arms are short. This chair is used for resting.

    director's chair Folding, usually wooden chair with legs that form *X*'s when open. The seat and back are canvas. The name is taken from movie directors who had their own such chairs stenciled with their names.

    folding chair Any chair which can be closed on itself. (This makes it easier to carry or to store.) Folding is accomplished in many different ways. Director's chairs, for instance, fold in the middle from arm to arm; folding chairs used for card games usually have seats which fold flat against the back. Folding chairs can be designed to resemble almost any style of furniture.

host and hostess chairs Armchairs made with wooden back and arms and lightly upholstered seats for use at the dining table. They are usually in the same style as the side chair.

recliner See *reclining chair.*

reclining chair Chair which can be moved from an upright position to a horizontal one by using a special mechanism. Reclining chairs usually offer a variety of positions and support for the feet. See chapter 8, "Buying Upholstered Furniture."

rocking chair Chair, usually made of wood, with curved pieces under the legs enabling the chair to move in a rocking motion.

side chair Chair designed for use at the sides of the dining table, made of wood, with a lightly upholstered seat and no arms.

sling chair Another name for *butterfly chair.*

Windsor chair Entirely wooden chair with curved back and arms. The back and arms are often supported by spokes of wood.

chest The term *chest* is used for two types of furniture — a box with a lid and a case with drawers. Following are descriptions of some of the many types of chests.

bachelor's chest Small chest of drawers designed to be used in a bedroom by one person.

blanket chest Long, low box with a lid in which blankets are kept. May be lined with cedar. See also *cedar chest.*

bureau A case with drawers usually larger and taller than a bachelor's chest and designed to hold clothing.

cedar chest Hinged, lidded box lined with cedar, a wood believed to repel moths, used to store woolens or as a hope chest. See also *hope chest.*

chest of drawers Term used to distinguish chests of the bureau type from lidded chests.

chest-on-chest Tall chest of drawers in two sections, often with the top section slightly smaller than the bottom.

highboy A tall chest of drawers with four legs for support.

hope chest Lidded chest used to store linens and other items in the hope of a future marriage.

lowboy Low chest of drawers on tablelike legs which raise it about two feet off the ground.

china Plates, cups, serving bowls, creamers, and so forth. The term correctly used applies only to pieces made from fine translucent earthenware or porcelain. Today, the term is often used as a generic term for a set of dishes.

china cabinet See *cabinet.*

chinoiserie (shee-nwaz-er-*ee*) French word used to describe a decorative or furniture style showing a Chinese influence. Highly lacquered cabinets, decorated with Chinese scenes and often accented in gold, are a feature of this style. See also *japan; Oriental.*

Chippendale Thomas Chippendale (1718-1779), English furniture maker, noted for chairs, including ladderback chairs. He used a great deal of mahogany and was influenced by many periods, including the Gothic and Chinese. The term *Chippendale* is used to describe furniture influenced by his work.

chrome See under *metal*.

chromium See under *metal*.

cigarette table See under *table*.

classic The word has two meanings. One refers to the period of the ancient Greeks and Romans characterized by columns and simple, often balanced, designs. It is used in this sense in such terms as *classic revival*, indicating a time of renewed interest in classical architecture and culture in the late eighteenth and early to mid-nineteenth centuries.

A classic is also anything which has stood the test of time. The word in this sense is used loosely of items developed as recently as five years ago.

closet Built-in storage area with a door, part of the structure of a house or apartment. Most closets have flat solid or hollow doors which open by means of hinges. *Sliding doors* can be useful for closets in rooms with limited floor space. *Walk-in closets* are closets large enough to walk into to hang or arrange stored items. *Louver doors* on closets may be desirable for air circulation. Closets should have lights. In damp climates, a light bulb left burning in a closet can impede the development of mildew. The bulb should be no more than 60 watts and placed well away from clothing to avoid the risk of fire.

cocktail table See *coffee table* under *table*.

coffee table See under *table*.

coil More or less interchangeable with *spring*, used in describing mattresses and box springs. See chapter 9, "Buying Bedding."

colonial Term used to describe furniture and decorating characteristic of the United States during the colonial period (prior to 1776).

color wheel A rainbowlike diagram in the shape of a circle used in decorating to select colors. Colors are considered contrasting or complementary according to their location on a color wheel. For a fuller discussion of color, see chapter 4, "Color, Texture, and Pattern."

compactor An appliance which compresses garbage and refuse electrically, so it occupies less space either in the home or when disposed of by a community. Caution should be used to avoid attracting insects and animals to compact garbage — compacting does not destroy germs.

console (*kon*-sole) See under *table*.

contemporary When the word *modern* (referring to architecture and furniture of the present day) became discredited as a result of a large number of poor designs, the word *contemporary* took its place. It means up to date and refers to whatever is the newest of styling. There is an implication of good taste.

contour In furniture, contouring usually refers to molding plastic so it fits the shape of the body, as in contoured chairs.

conversation area A section of a room where conversation can take place. It usually consists of at least a sofa and two chairs. A *conversation group* is a grouping of furniture (usually the above) arranged to make talking easy. A *conversation pit* is a sunken section of a room, often with upholstered or carpeted steps leading to it so that people can sit on the edge to talk.

cork See *resilient flooring.*

corner block See chapter 6, "Buying Wood Furniture."

corner cupboards Corner cupboards are a practical solution to the corner problem. They are pieces of furniture designed to hold and display such things as books or (more often) china; they often have glass doors in the top half, shelves throughout. The back of a corner cupboard fits into the corner, the front is on a diagonal. The cupboard forms a right triangle. Corner cupboards may be built in or bought as furniture.

corners Corners are a problem in decorating. Whenever something joins something else (bookshelves, kitchen cabinets) at the corner, the corner is more or less lost. In kitchen cabinets this can be overcome by use of a lazy Susan designed to revolve and make access to items in the corner possible. In sectional furniture where sofa and chair sections turn corners, the corner seat is lost. Corner tables, placed between the sections of sectional furniture, often prove more useful — they can be reached from either section. See also *sectional furniture.*

cornice See section on molding in chapter 12, "Room Backgrounds."

couch See *sofa.*

country See *provincial.*

counter Long, flat surface, often topping a cabinet and used for working, dining, and so forth.

cozy corner Term used in the late nineteenth century for a corner of a room heaped high with pillows, often closed off from the rest of the room by draperies, to make a comfortable small sitting area.

cubbyhole Small, usually rectangular storage place. In schools, cubbyholes are usually square, labeled with children's names, and often abbreviated to "cubby." In a home, a cubbyhole can be any space where various objects can be placed for tidiness.

cube Three-dimensional square. Cubes have become popular as furniture has become more modular. Cubes are made with shelves, with spaces to hold records, with doors, or entirely open. They can be plastic, wood, or any other material and are usually designed so that they can be stacked to make a storage wall. See *sectional furniture; storage wall.*

curio See *bric-a-brac.*

curtains and draperies *Curtains* are window coverings — usually not lined — which hang inside the window, more or less against the glass. They usually end at the windowsill. *Draperies* are almost always lined, usually hang outside the window frame, and are often made of very heavy, luxurious materials. Draperies are usually floor length but occasionally lie on the floor itself or end a few inches above the floor. Following are definitions of a few terms commonly used. For a fuller discussion, see chapter 10, "Window Treatments."

café curtains   Curtains hung in tiers so one row covers the top of a window, the other the bottom half. Other variations are possible.

draw draperies   Draperies which can be closed or opened, usually by means of cords.

glass curtains   Sheer curtains hung inside the window, just covering the glass. Also called *under curtains*. Do not confuse with *glass fiber curtains*. See *glass fiber*.

tieback curtains   Curtains held to the side of a window by a tieback. See also *tieback*.

cushion   See *pillow*.

D

dado (*day*-do) See section on molding in chapter 12, "Room Backgrounds."

davenport See under *sofa*.

deacon's bench See *bench; settle*.

den See *study*.

desk Piece of furniture with a flat or occasionally sloping surface for working and writing. Desks usually but not always contain drawers. They may be made from almost any material including glass, wood, metal, and plastic; the top of the desk may be covered with leather or another material. A *lady's desk* is a small desk, often with delicate decoration, found both as an antique and as a reproduction.

dimmer Electrical device which, when connected to the lighting system at a wall switch, enables incandescent lights to be dimmed to lower than their usual level. The technical name is rheostat. See also chapter 13, "Planning Your Lighting."

dining area Section of a room (usually a living room) set off from the rest of the room either architecturally, such as an alcove, or by decoration, which serves as a place to eat.

dining room Room devoted primarily to eating. Dining rooms are usually (not always) large enough for twelve people to sit in comfort at a dining table.

director's chair See under *chair*.

dishwasher Automatic machine (the word *electric* is understood) which rinses, washes, rinses, and dries dishes which have been used for eating or cooking. Dishwashers are not within the scope of this book but space for them must be included in planning a kitchen. They usually require running water, drainage, and electricity.

distressed finish Artificially created appearance of age. For example, a distressed finish can be made by spilling ink on new furniture, hammering nails in it to resemble worm holes, and hitting the furniture with hammers. See chapter 6, "Buying Wood Furniture."

doodad See *bric-a-brac*.

door knocker Metal object fastened to a door to enable a person to make a louder noise than possible by rapping with bare knuckles in order to alert those inside to the presence of someone outside. Door knockers are often made of brass, with or without a clear finish to delay tarnishing. Excellent reproductions of antique door knockers are widely available.

dormer Projecting upright window in a slanting roof. See also chapter 10, "Window Treatments."

double dresser Mid-height chest of drawers with two rows of drawers arranged side by side. See also *chest*.

draperies See *curtains and draperies*.

draw draperies See *curtains and draperies*.

drawer pull See *pulls*.

drawers Rectangular boxes with open tops. Drawers are drawn out of a piece of furniture, hence the name. Secret drawers are found in some old pieces of furniture and in modern reproductions.

drawing room See *living room*.

dressing table See under *table*.

drop leaf table See under *table*.

dry sink Dry sinks were sinks (places where water could be held for washing of various kinds) without running water. They were often made of wood lined with metal in the sink section, stood waist high, and had cupboards beneath and sometimes shelves above. Today, antique dry sinks and copies of these are used for a variety of purposes, from bars to planters. See also *planter*.

E

early American See chart, chapter 5, "What is Period Furniture?"

Eastern In the sense it is used in decorating, *Eastern* usually refers to items from the Orient or inspired by the Orient. On occasion, the term may refer to items from the Middle East, such as Egypt or Iran (Persia). See also *chinoiserie*; *Oriental*.

eclectic Literally, this term refers to borrowing from many different sources. In decorating, it refers to mixing periods. This was once taboo but it is now both popular and acceptable.

eighteenth-century furniture See chart, chapter 5, "What Is Period Furniture?".

Elizabethan Dark, heavy furniture made of oak, in deep colors. Named for Elizabeth I of England, who reigned from 1558 to 1603. Jacobean and Tudor furniture and decoration are similar, as is Spanish of the same period. See chart, chapter 5, "What Is Period Furniture?"

ell See *L-shaped*.

end table See under *table*.

escritoire (es-kree-*twar*) French for "writing desk." See *secretary*.

étagère French word for a set of shelves. Describes a piece of furniture, usually pyramid or square, sometimes with all four sides open, built with a series of shelves used to display bric-a-brac and other items.

extension table See under *table*.

F

facing (1) A fabric facing backs up (faces) other fabric. It usually finishes a raw edge and adds support to the outside material. Facings are used in home decorating on curtains, slipcovers, and upholstery. (2) A fireplace facing is the decorative edge around the fireplace opening, usually called the mantel. See *mantel*.

family room Current term for an extra room in the house, less formal than most living rooms, designed for relaxing, entertaining, and games. Formerly known as the game room or the rumpus room, the family room reflects the recurring need for a room where people can make a mess.

Federal See chart, chapter 5, "What Is Period Furniture?"

fiber glass See *glass fiber*.

fiberfill Man-made (often polyester) fluffy material often used in making furniture. Fiberfill, unlike foam, attempts to imitate feathers or down in softness.

finial Decorative object at the top of peaked roofs, bed posts, fences, and so forth. Finials rise above the plane of the rest of the item and may be either abstract designs or representations of objects from nature. Pineapples and eagles are popular designs for finials.

finishing The final touch in the manufacture of wood furniture. See chapter 6, "Buying Wood Furniture."

fixture Anything which is permanently attached to a building. Bathroom fixtures, for instance, include the sink and bathtub; a lighting fixture is attached to the ceiling or wall, in contrast to a lamp, which can be moved.

flatware See *silverware*.

flip-top See *tilt-top table* under *table*.

floorboards Floorboards, also called *flooring* or *wood flooring*, are pieces of wood (often oak) joined together tightly and nailed either to other boards underneath or to the beams supporting the building. Floorboards can be any

220

width, from the narrow boards of most new flooring to the wide random-width boards of early American and early American-style houses.

flooring Any material which covers the floor of a room. The term can include carpets and rugs but in practice usually does not. It is often used to refer to materials that can be added after a building is completed. The word tends to imply a hard surface such as vinyl. See also *resilient flooring* and chapter 12, "Room Backgrounds."

floor lamp See under *lamp.*

focal point One of the basic beliefs of decorating is that every room should have a focal point—a major attention-getter. In many living rooms this will be a fireplace, since fireplaces tend to dominate both the wall they are on and the room they are in. A focal point can be almost anything—a breakfront, a painting, or a display of a china collection.

folding chair See under *chair.*

folding rule See *carpenter's rule.*

four-poster See under *bed.*

free form A non-geometric shape. The term is used in modern furniture to describe, for instance, a coffee table of no definable shape but rather drawn or cut in a loose form.

French provincial See chart, chapter 5, "What Is Period Furniture?" See also *Italian provincial*, same chart.

fruitwood Any wood from a fruit-bearing tree. As used today by the furniture industry, the term generally refers to a stain used to make less desirable wood resemble one of the fruit trees, such as cherry. When furniture is made of solid or veneered wood from a fruit tree, the name of the wood (cherry, for instance) is almost always used.

furniture Any movable item in a building. Usually the term refers only to wooden and upholstered pieces, although it can also refer to metal filing cabinets. See individual sections on various types of furniture for detailed information.

furring strips Strips of wood nailed to a wall or other surface in preparation for something else being attached to them. Wood panelling can often be nailed directly to a wall in good condition; a wall in bad condition, however, should have furring strips attached and the wood panelling nailed to them.

G

game room See *family room*.

girandole A branched candlestick. The term has also come to be used to indicate a pair of antique candlesticks, often hung with glass cut to reflect the light.

glass curtains See under *curtains and draperies*.

glass fiber Fiber made from glass and used extensively for curtains and draperies. It is also used to give additional strength to polyester plastic furniture. Glass fiber fabrics are strong and wash well but should be washed by hand to avoid leaving splinters of glass in the washing machine. Care, of course, should be taken to protect the hands. Glass fiber has poor resistance to abrasion but is fireproof.

glassware Any object made of glass, including, for instance, a mirror. Usually, however, the term is used in decorating for such items as drinking glasses, vases, and glass plates.

Gothic Refers to the pointed arch style in European architecture from the twelfth to the sixteenth centuries. Cathedrals are the best-known examples. Some furniture (notably church furniture such as the pews) repeats the characteristic soaring lines and pointed arches of this period.

Gothic revival Period during the nineteenth century when elements of Gothic design were reinterpreted in both public and domestic architecture and furniture. Stained glass windows in homes are one example of the revival.

guest room When most houses were larger than today's average home the guest room — also known as the *best room* or *spare room* — was furnished as a bedroom and reserved solely for guests. It was often better furnished than the rest of the house. Today, guest rooms are often made into studies, extra sitting or living rooms, or sewing rooms with a sofa bed for the occasional guest.

gumwood Plentiful strong native American hardwood extensively used in furniture manufacturing but almost never identified by name. See chapter 6, "Buying Wood Furniture."

H

habitat Literally, in French, "living condition." Because of various uses of this word in recent years, its meaning has broadened and it is now associated with the best in contemporary design. An exhibit of prophetic housing at the 1967 Montreal World's Fair (Expo) was called Habitat. The United Nations has held conferences about habitat and there are stores in Europe and Great Britain with the name.

half-timber Usually applied to Elizabethan and Tudor architecture, it refers to a wall consisting half of wood and half of plaster. The same effect is seen from the inside and the outside.

hanging basket A basket suspended, usually by string or leather thongs, from a high point. Hanging baskets have recently become popular for holding potted plants, especially trailing vines. The strings and occasionally the basket itself are often made of macrame (string tied in intricate knots).

hanging See *wall hanging*.

hard goods Department store and manufacturing term used to distinguish between textile (soft goods) and non-textile items. Upholstered furniture, even though it is soft, is considered hard goods.

hardware In furniture, hardware means small metal items, such as those used on wood furniture — hinges, knobs, drawer pulls, and so forth. Although some furniture hardware is made of china, glass, and plastic it is still called hardware. Brass is probably the most popular metal for hardware. See under *metal*.

hardwood Term used to distinguish wood of certain trees from the wood of other trees. The name *hardwood* has nothing to do with the strength of the wood. Hardwood is wood from deciduous trees (trees that shed their leaves every year in temperate climates); softwood comes from evergreen trees. See chapter 6, "Buying Wood Furniture."

hassock See *ottoman*.

headboard See *bed*.

Hepplewhite George Hepplewhite, English furniture maker of the late eighteenth century, noted for chairs, especially the shield-back design, still

223

available in mass-produced furniture today. His furniture (or furniture attributed to him) used mahogany, with inlays of exotic woods. Small tables, cabinets, desks, and sideboards are also attributed to him.

highboy See under *chest.*

hinge A flexible device — in furniture, almost always metal — which allows one section of an item, such as a door, to swing while the rest remains still.

holdback See *tieback.*

home furnishings Everything which fills and decorates a home and can be removed. Bathroom fixtures, for instance, are not considered home furnishings; desks, bedding, curtains, and lamps are. It originated as a department store and industry term but is now coming into more general use.

hooked rug See under *rugs and carpets.*

hope chest See under *chest.*

host and hostess chairs See under *chair.*

hot tray Flat surface, usually glass heated by electricity, which keeps food at a constant temperature. See also *serving cart.*

hurricane lamp See under *lamp.*

hutch Piece of furniture placed or joined on top of another piece. The bottom section usually has drawers; the hutch top usually has open shelves. Hutches can be used for holding china in a dining room, books in a den or bedroom.

I

Indian Refers to two different groups of people — natives of India, the country in Asia, and the original pre-European inhabitants of North, South, and Central America. The influence of Indian Indian design is seen especially in colors and fabrics. Gauze fabrics from India are currently popular for clothing and curtains. North American Indian influences in decorating have been limited mainly to blanket and rug patterns, often characterized by bright color and geometric or stylized animal motifs. South and Central American Indian influences on decorating trends have been stronger and longer lasting; they include not only design elements but also certain building materials (adobe, a type of baked clay, for example) for homes. Their influence is especially strong in the southwestern United States.

indoor-outdoor carpeting See under *rugs and carpets*.

Italian provincial See chart, Chapter 5, "What Is Period Furniture?"

J

jabot (zhah-*bo*) Decorative ruffled fabric placed over a window, usually used with curtains or draperies. See also *swag*.

Jacobean See chart, chapter 5, "What Is Period Furniture?"

japan When *japan* is spelled with a small *j*, it refers to an extremely hard varnish which was originally introduced to Europe from Japan. The varnish was used for furniture on which gold was used to decorate the wood with Oriental scenes. See also *chinoiserie*; *Oriental*.

K

king-size bed See under *bed*.

kitchenware Utensils used in a kitchen for cooking — pots, pans, and so forth. Occasionally, the term is also used for dishes which are informal and used only in the kitchen.

kit Set of objects to be assembled into a finished item. Kits for making unfinished furniture are now available. They are obtainable by mail and contain complete instructions, nails, and adhesives, and anything else needed to put the furniture together. Styles range from modern to antique. Kits are also available for finished furniture.

knot Dark marking on a piece of wood, usually indicating where a branch once grew. Depending on the effect desired, knots are considered either attractive or unattractive. Rustic and provincial furniture are more likely to incorporate knots as part of the design than is more formal furniture. Knots tend to be weaker than other parts of pieces of wood and may pop out if used in panelling. A *burl* has much the same look as a knot but the term implies something much more attractive. Burls are usually larger than knots and come from a variety of causes. Burls are often made part of the design of a piece of formal wood furniture by being placed in a conspicuous place such as the center of a coffee table.

L

L-shaped Formed like the Letter *L*. A fairly common shape for living rooms, with one long section and a short section at right angles to it. The shorter section is often used as a dining area or sleeping alcove. *L* is sometimes spelled *ell*.

lacquer See *paints, lacquers, and varnishes.*

lady's desk See under *desk*.

lambrequin Structure at the top and sides of window, framing the window and usually part of the window decoration. It is often made of wood and may be covered with fabric or paint.

lamp Anything used to provide light. In decorating, lamps are usually electric and can be moved from one room to another or one part of a room to another. Following are descriptions of some types of lamps.

chandelier See *hanging lamp.*

floor lamp Stands on its own base rather than on a table or desk. Other names for floor lamps include *bridge lamp* and *standing lamp.*

gooseneck lamp Has a flexible section between the base and the shade, enabling the lamp to be bent in various directions. Gooseneck lamps are usually table lamps but may also be floor lamps.

hanging lamp Suspended, usually from the ceiling, rather than resting with its base on the ceiling or floor. Chandeliers are hanging lamps, usually having many different bulbs and a certain amount of decoration designed to resemble candles, which lighted the original chandeliers. The word comes from the French for *candle.* Modern hanging lamps usually consist of one bulb with the light directed downward by an opaque shade.

high intensity lamp Designed for use with special bulbs which provide greater illumination than normal incandescent bulbs. High intensity lamps are normally used for studying and reading or close work.

hurricane lamp Most often used with a candle or kerosene. Designed with a sturdy, protective chimney (usually glass) which covers the flame

228

to keep it from being blown out in the wind. Hurricane lamps have heavy bases to prevent their being blown over.

standing lamp See *floor lamp.*

study lamp Designed to rest on a desk and illuminate work. Study lamps usually have light directed toward the surface of a desk rather than providing general illumination as do table lamps. Other types of lamps, such as gooseneck and high intensity, are often used for studying.

table lamp Rests on a table (usually a table the height of the arm of an upholstered chair). The shade is most often translucent so that the lamp can provide both general lighting and light for reading.

Tiffany lamp Any one of a series of elaborately decorated Art Nouveau lamps designed by Louis Comfort Tiffany (1848-1933). The term is also used for reproductions and adaptations of these. The original lamps often had shades made of stained glass in flowing floral shapes.

latex paint See *paints, lacquers, and varnishes.*

lattice Open framework made of strips of wood, metal, or other material woven in and out. Lattices are used to support vines and other plants. They are often used without plants as decorative accents.

lazy Susan Round tray set on a base which remains stationary while the tray revolves. Lazy Susans are used in the center of dining tables to hold condiments and are also useful in corners of cupboards.

leaded glass Glass, usually cut into designed shapes, held together by strips of lead. Sometimes but not always correctly called *stained glass.*

library See *study.*

light bulb Bulb-shaped (somewhat rounded at the base) glass object which, through the heating filament, creates incandescent light. The quality of light obtained from a lamp or fixture is determined by the light bulb used in it. The term is also occasionally applied incorrectly to fluorescent lighting devices, most of which are actually tubes. See also chapter 13, "Planning Your Lighting."

linen-fold Type of carving on wood, usually decorating the front of furniture. It resembles unstitched fabric tucks.

living room Room designed for sitting, entertaining, and relaxing. Although usually more formal than a family room, a living room can be as formal or informal as desired. Also called *drawing room, sitting room, parlor, lounge.*

love seat Small sofa which seats two people. Some love seats are designed without arms. Much armless upholstered furniture is meant to be used as part of a sectional furniture layout; it can be moved to work on its own, however. See also *sectional furniture; sofa.*

lowboy See under *chest.*

Lucite DuPont trade name for acrylic plastic. See *acrylic plastic.*

M

man-made In home decorating, the term is used to refer to anything which is chemically created and therefore not found naturally. Included are fibers (made into fabrics or filling for upholstery), plastics both hard (acrylic plastic used for tables) and soft (polyurethane foam used in mattresses), and various types of floor coverings, such as the vinyls. The development of these products has revolutionized both the manufacture and the care of home furnishings. See also *plastic*.

make-up table See *dressing table* under *table*.

mantel The facing around a fireplace. Mantels are made of wood, brick, marble, stone, or other material. The mantel usually includes the mantelpiece (shelf of the mantel over the fireplace opening).

mantelpiece See *mantel*.

masonry Term usually used for stone or brick joined by cement. It may also be used for cement or concrete walls or blocks. In home decoration the term is used in connection with installation of items on walls and with the use of paint.

mat A border between the frame of a picture and the picture itself, designed to give additional emphasis to the picture. Mats are often white but may be any color or material.

matchstick blinds See *venetian blinds* under *shades and blinds*.

mattress A rectangular fabric case filled with a soft material and used as a cushion for resting and sleeping. For a fuller discussion of the many types of mattresses available, see chapter 9, "Buying Bedding."

Mediterranean Industry name for a recently developed style of furniture in very dark-toned woods with a certain solid look, designed to imitate the furniture of seventeenth-century Spain. It is similar in mood to Elizabethan, Tudor, and Jacobean styles. See chart, chapter 5, "What Is Period Furniture?"

metal Used in home furnishings for many purposes, from curtain rods to furniture. The following is a list of some of the most common metals and their characteristics. Metals are used on their own or combined with other metals to form alloys.

aluminum Lightweight, naturally silvery, rust-free metal; relatively expensive.

brass Alloy of copper, zinc, and other metals. Naturally gold in color, tarnishes and requires polishing.

chrome Silvery coating of chromium applied to other metals (for instance, brass). Does not tarnish or require polishing; benefits from washing and drying.

chromium Hard metal used with other metals to harden them or increase their wearing qualities.

stainless steel Steel alloyed with chromium or another metal to resist corrosion.

steel Strong alloy of iron and carbon; affected by corrosion.

wrought iron Iron used extensively in furniture; usually black; may rust.

mix-and-match Term used for coordinated furniture, fabric, rugs, and so forth to indicate to the customer that items can be either matched or unmatched in any customer-selected assortment.

modern Something which is considered up-to-date. In furniture, *modern* usually implies very plain lines and often the use of man-made materials. See also *contemporary.*

modular See *sectional furniture.*

molding An edging, usually decorative, generally made of wood, which finishes or accents furniture or walls. See section on molding, chapter 12, "Room Backgrounds."

monochromatic Strictly speaking, the term *monochromatic* means different tints (light, medium, dark) of one color used together. A monochromatic room, however, often also includes colors on either side of the main color on a color wheel.

motif (mo-*teef*) Any kind of design. A motif is often small, as in a fabric with a leaf motif, or attached separately, as when a piece of furniture has a lion's head motif.

nail See *screws*.

nailhead Rounded, decorative, metal trimming for upholstery. Nailheads are usually inserted individually in a row along the edges of upholstered furniture.

nap Fuzzy, soft, or hairlike surface of any fabric, including rugs and carpets.

Naugahyde Uniroyal trade name for vinyl. See under *vinyl plastic*.

neutral colors Colors which can be used with many other colors because they blend easily and well. Black, brown, gray, beige, and white are the colors most commonly considered neutrals.

nightstand See *end table* under *table*.

O

occasional furniture Wood furniture such as tables and some chairs. See also discussion of furniture terminology in chapter 17, "Getting What You Want."

occasional table See *occasional furniture*.

olefin Generic name for fiber made from polypropylene or polyethylene. Olefin resists chemicals, mildew, and weather and is important in home furnishings for relatively inexpensive rugs and upholstery. Occasionally called *polypropylene*.

Oriental Term can apply to many different things from architecture to floor coverings. Oriental architecture and furniture when reinterpreted for use in the West usually features straight lines and, in the case of furniture, is lower than usual. Other Oriental furniture includes elaborately lacquered (japanned) and decorated wood furniture. Oriental rugs are handmade rugs produced in the Middle and Far East either by hand-weaving or hand-knotting. See also *japan*; *chinoiserie*; *Eastern*.

ottoman Low, upholstered piece of furniture without back or arms. It can be used for sitting or to support the feet. Also called a *hassock* or *pouf*.

outdoor furniture See *summer furniture*.

P

padding Any layer, usually of fabric, placed under other fabric to support it, provide additional comfort, and increase wearing ability. Padding is used in upholstered furniture. Carpet padding made of cattle hair, rubberized hair, rubber, jute and cattle hair, or man-made materials is used to increase the life and luxury of rugs and carpets. Padding is also called *cushion* and *underlay*. See also *rugs and carpets*.

paints, lacquers, and varnishes Substances used to protect and enhance a surface. Recently developed man-made materials have changed traditional paints, lacquers, and varnishes, their application, and their care. Plastic lacquers are now available which render a surface almost impervious to traditional enemies such as water. Paints have been developed which are quick-drying and almost odor-free. For a full discussion, see chapters 6 and 12, "Buying Wood Furniture" and "Room Backgrounds."

parlor See *living room*.

Parsons table See under *table*.

patio furniture See *summer furniture*.

pattern Any repeated design. A pattern on fabric or wallpaper is usually repeated at least once every yard. The repeat of a pattern is important in home decorating. See also *repeat*; chapter 4, "Color, Texture, and Pattern."

pedestal table See under *table*.

pegboard A man-made flat surface covered with small regular holes. Special hooks and other attachments fit into the holes. Pegboard is used to cover walls for storage. It has a certain sound-controlling quality because the holes absorb some of the sound waves. Pegboard is difficult to clean and sometimes attracts insects which move into the holes.

Pennsylvania Dutch A term referring to a group of German settlers in Pennsylvania and their descendants, belonging mainly to the Mennonite religion. The Amish are the best known of the Pennsylvania Dutch groups although not the largest. Pennsylvania Dutch furniture and decorative items are characterized by a rustic quality including painted decorative finishes in primary colors. These often use hex signs (symbolic, stylized, often geometric forms designed to ward off evil) and hearts and flowers as motifs.

Phyfe Duncan Phyfe (1768-1854), American (Scottish immigrant) furniture maker who worked in mahogany. Noted for his use of the lyre shape and pedestal tables. Many of his designs are available in adaptations from mass furniture producers.

pie crust Decorative edging used on some traditional tables (usually round ones). It resembles the edge of a pie which has been pinched by the fingers, giving a scalloped effect.

pillow Fabric case filled with some type of soft material — feathers, down, rags, foam, foam chips — and closed. *Cushions* are usually somewhat firmer than pillows and are used on upholstered furniture. See chapter 8, "Buying Upholstered Furniture."

plant stand Stand designed to hold plants. Styles range from purely functional tiered metal stands obtainable from ten-cent and garden supply stores to elaborate open stands made of a series of shelves. See also *étagère*.

planter Anything that holds a plant. In furniture, the term implies a metal-lined hole to hold soil for plants to grow in.

plastic An organic, synthetic, or processed material which can be molded and is often used in furniture. See chapter 7, "Buying Today's New Furniture."

Following is a list of some of the most commonly used plastics.

ABS Shiny, hard, rigid, opaque. Softens and melts under concentrated heat. Withstands heavy blows. Found in all types of case goods and occasional furniture.

acrylic Clear or colored, it is also available in translucent and opaque forms; loses shape in boiling water, melts under flame; scratches easily and looks cloudy when scratched; used in many types of case goods, occasional furniture; also as glass substitute in doors.

melamine Clear or colored, available either translucent or opaque, discolors or chars when exposed to temperature over 210° Fahrenheit (99° Centigrade); used on furniture tops and fronts (laminated).

nylon Varying degrees of transparency and opacity available; resists extremes of temperature; stained by coffee, dyes; used primarily to replace wood in such items as drawer glides.

olefin See *polyolefin*.

polyester Transparent to translucent; almost always used with glass fiber for strength; can be fire resistant; damaged by hard blows; used alone for decorative motifs on wood furniture; used with glass fiber for tables, chairs, and upholstered furniture frames.

polyolefin Somewhat translucent; melts under heat and flame; resists scratching; used for seating (then often called polypropionate.).

polystyrene Usually translucent, can be opaque; often colored and textured to resemble wood; burns slowly under direct flame; strong, may be brittle; found in occasional furniture, often in imitation of wood carving; also used for upholstered furniture frames.

polyurethane Spongy, either rigid or flexible, naturally cream in color, darkens on exposure to air but does not deteriorate; used for upholstery cushioning in flexible form and for upholstered furniture frames and fronts of drawers in rigid form.

vinyl Fabriclike; available clear, translucent, or opaque; avoid heat and flame; strong but can be scratched and torn; used for upholstery fabric, furniture such as water beds.

Plexiglas Rohm and Haas trade name for acrylic plastic. See also *acrylic plastic*.

plush Fabric with an unusually long nap. See also *rugs and carpets*.

plywood Layers of wood joined together with grains at right angles, resulting in a strong material. Can be molded. See also chapter 6, "Buying Wood Furniture."

pouf Very puffy down or synthetic fiber-filled bedspread or quilt used on a bed. Also another name for *ottoman*. See *ottoman*.

prepasted vinyl See *wall covering*.

prepasted wallpaper See *wallpaper*.

provincial Pertaining to the provinces (rather than the capital city) of a country and, in home decorating, a word used interchangeably with *country* and *rustic*. Provincial styling is usually less formal than urban styling. See also chapter 5, "What Is Period Furniture?"

pulls Objects, usually made of metal, although occasionally of wood, china, or plastic, placed on the front of furniture pieces in order to pull open drawers, desk covers, etc. Pulls are also called *knobs*. See also *hardware*.

Q

Queen Anne See chart, chapter 5, "What Is Period Furniture?"
queen-size bed See under *bed*.

R

ranch style Popular post-World War II house design featuring one-story construction.

rattan See *cane*.

recliner See *reclining chair* under *chair*.

Régence (ray-*zhans*) See chart, chapter 5, "What Is Period Furniture?"

Regency See chart, chapter 5, "What Is Period Furniture?"

repeat Design which occurs over and over on fabric or wallpaper, and the amount of space taken by this design before it begins again. Since designs should be centered on sofas and aligned on wallpapers, it is desirable to know the size of the repeat to determine yardage requirements. The larger the pattern, the larger the repeat.

reproduction Faithful copy, usually of an antique piece of furniture. An *adaptation* is furniture made smaller, lighter, lower, or using different materials from the original to suit current taste.

resilient flooring Term used for man-made floorings (such as vinyl) which are available in sheets or in tile form. Cork is often included, although, because it is difficult to keep clean, it is rarely used. For a fuller discussion, see chapter 12, "Room Backgrounds."

rheostat See *dimmer*.

rings Growth marks on trees which eventually become part of the surface design of furniture. Also marks indicating damage on wood furniture, usually from wet glasses.

rocker See *rocking chair* under *chair*.

rug pad See *padding*.

rugs and carpets Often used interchangeably, although a *rug* usually does not cover the entire floor and is not fastened to it, while a *carpet* covers the entire floor and is fastened to it. Following is a description of some common kinds of rugs.

area rug Small usually decorative rug often used as an accent or to separate a section of a room from the rest.

broadloom Carpet woven on a loom at least nine feet wide. Also used of wide tufted carpeting. See *tufted rug*.

hand-knotted rug Handworked rugs, including Oriental and Persian rugs, which are among the most expensive made. The more knots to the inch, the finer the rug.

hooked rug Rug made by hand or machine using a hook to pull yarn through a backing. Hooked rugs are increasingly popular as a do-it-yourself activity, and often end up as wall hangings. See also *wall hanging*.

indoor-outdoor carpeting Carpeting, usually made of olefin, a weather-resistant fiber, which can be used outdoors as well as inside.

loop rug Rug with an uncut loop pile. Loops may vary in height, be all the same height, or be random sheared, where some loops are cut and others are uncut.

narrow carpet Carpet made on a loom about three feet wide. The term is used to distinguish it from broadloom. Narrow carpet is often used on stairways.

Oriental rug Handmade rug from the Middle or Far East, handwoven or hand-knotted.

Persian rug Oriental rug made in Iran. See *Oriental rug*.

rag rug Rug woven of strips of fabric on a cotton or synthetic yarn backing. Rag rugs are made by hand or machine and are usually quite inexpensive. *Braided rugs* are made of rags braided into long strips, then wound around and sewn together, usually in a circle or oval.

rya rug (*ry*-ah) Scandinavian shag rug, usually dramatic in color. Best quality are hand-knotted.

shag rug, or shag carpet Rug or carpet with an extremely long pile.

tufted rug The most common type of rug construction. Machine needles rapidly push yarn into rug backing to form a pile which can be looped, cut, or sheared.

woven rug A rug made by weaving (taking yarn over and under other yarn at right angles).

rumpus room See *family room*.

rung Piece of wood, usually rounded, placed between the legs of a chair to provide additional support. Rungs are also found on the backs of some wooden chairs and as steps for ladders, including those used with bunk beds. Metal chairs have metal rungs.

rustic See *provincial*.

S

sandpaper Paper with real or synthetic sand bonded to it, used in finishing furniture and wood. Sanding is one of the first steps in finishing. Begin with the coarsest grade of sandpaper; as the surface becomes smoother, advance to the finest grade. Sandpaper is useful for trimming edges of sticking doors slightly and smoothing splinters in already finished furniture. Sandpaper can be purchased in many stores, including ten-cent stores, hardware stores, and home centers.

screws Cylinder-shaped, usually metal, objects used to fasten things together. Screws have ridges to help them hold; nails are straight up and down. Screws are more satisfactory than nails for furniture when holding ability is even moderately important. See chapter 6, "Buying Wood Furniture," for the use of screws in wood furniture and chapter 14, "Finishing Touches," for screws suitable for use in hanging objects on walls.

scrubbable A term which implies that an item, usually a wall covering, can take more vigorous cleaning — with, for instance, an abrasive cleanser — than the term *washable* implies. Scrubbable paints and wallpapers are available. In the case of paint, it is important to wait the time indicated by the manufacturer (often as long as thirty days) before scrubbing.

secretary Writing desk with drawers and a deck above the desk area with glass or wood doors which can hold books and other items. Also called an *escritoire*.

sectional furniture Furniture made in sections which can be combined as desired by the customer. The term is usually used for upholstered furniture; wood or plastic furniture of this type is called modular. A customer can make a sofa by combining one left-handed and one right-handed armchair and any number of armless chairs or love seats for the middle section.

semanier (se-mah-*nyay*) From the French for week (semain), a *semanier* is a tall, narrow chest of drawers. It should have seven drawers — one for each day of the week—but the term is used for chests with other numbers of drawers.

serving cart Two-shelved piece of furniture with a handle at one end and wheels or casters on the legs. A serving cart can be loaded with dishes and food in one area and wheeled to another. Serving carts which have a heating element (*hot tray*) in the top are available. Such hot trays must, of course, be plugged into an electric outlet. *Tea cart* is another name for a serving cart. See also *hot tray*.

settee Any kind of sofa or double chair, often with a wood frame. See also *sofa*.

settle Bench with high back and arms, usually made of wood and having a chest under the seat. Also called a *deacon's bench*.

shades and blinds The terms *shades* and *blinds* are used more or less interchangeably. Both are decorative and provide privacy and light control. Following are some of the more important types.

Austrian shades Shades made of fabric shirred across the width. When drawn up, Austrian shades hang in graceful loops.

roller blinds Shades which wind around a roller or dowel to expose the window. These shades are available in colors and can be made to match or coordinate with fabrics in the room.

Roman shades Similar to Austrian shades; however, when Roman shades are down they hang straight while Austrian shades remain shirred.

venetian blinds Blinds made of strips of fabric, metal, or plastic, which can be raised or lowered in one piece; the slats can be tilted to shut out light or opened to filter in light. *Matchstick blinds* are similar, but with much narrower slats. Sometimes they are only controlled by rolling onto themselves, rather than having individually movable slats.

shaving mirror Small mirror which stands by itself on top of a table or chest.

shelving See *bookcase*.

Sheraton Thomas Sheraton (1751-1806): cabinetmaker known for fancy work, often with secret drawers. He used a great deal of satinwood (a tropical wood), veneers, and inlays.

shutters Hinged wooden panels used to cover windows or doors. Shutters have recently returned to popularity in decorating. They are available solid, with open panels (into which fabric or plastic can be inserted), and with movable or fixed louvers (overlapping strips of wood). Louvered shutter doors can be used on closets to ensure air circulation.

side chair See under *chair*.

sideboard Table or (more often) flat-topped chest placed at the side of a dining room for serving. See also *buffet*.

silver cloth Fabric permeated with a substance which inhibits tarnish from forming on silver. Some buffets have drawers lined with silver cloth. Silver cloth is made into cases to hold silver utensils and bags to hold silver serving dishes. Kits are also available to be used in lining drawers with silver cloth.

silverware Correctly, sterling silver or silver-plated eating utensils. Term is also used for non-silver eating utensils such as stainless steel. The industry term for all eating utensils is *flatware*.

sleep sofa A sofa which can be changed into a bed. See chapter 9, "Buying Bedding."

slipcovers Unattached fabric coverings for upholstered furniture. They are made with openings so they can be easily removed for cleaning or changing.

sofa Upholstered piece of furniture having a raised back and arms which seats three or more people at one time. A *couch* may have no back and arms, or only a back. *Davenport* is another name for a large sofa. See also *sectional furniture; love seat; sofa bed;* chapter 8, "Buying Upholstered Furniture."

soundproofing Term used to describe treating and furnishing a room to exclude external sound. Complete soundproofing cannot be achieved in the home, but many of the techniques listed in the section on sound in chapter 12, "Room Backgrounds" and many of the energy-saving techniques mentioned in chapter 16, "Saving Energy," will help muffle outside sound.

Spanish Term used to refer to furniture of the kind brought to Mexico and parts of the United States by early Spanish explorers and missionaries. Furniture is heavy, bulky, often intricately carved with open spaces in the designs, and made of dark wood. See also chart, chapter 5, "What Is Period Furniture?"

spare room See *guest room*.

spice shelf Small, occasionally tiered shelf for holding spices.

stained glass Decorative colored glass used in windows and occasionally for lamp shades. The glass filters light and usually cannot be seen through. Recently, stained glass, used sparingly, has been returning to popularity in American homes.

stains See various sections for care of stained items; also see *paints, lacquers, and varnishes*.

standing lamp See *floor lamp* under *lamp*.

stencil Pattern on stiff cardboard or metal for copying a design. The desired design is cut into the card or metal, and paint or other coloring is put through the holes. Stencil designs were a popular way of decorating walls in early American times and are a characteristic decoration of Pennsylvania Dutch furniture.

stool Seat for one person, usually made of wood, with three or more legs, often backless. A *step stool* is a short ladder which usually opens to form a triangle for support. A *footstool* is a small, low, usually upholstered benchlike object for resting the feet.

storage wall Wall covered with shelves, hanging cabinets, standing cabinets, and so forth. Many wall storage systems are sectional — also called modular — in design, so that you can choose the components you desire. A living room storage wall, for instance, might contain a bar, record cabinets, bookshelves, record player, television set, and a display of plants. A bedroom storage wall could include hanging space for clothing, a small desk or dressing table, and cupboards for sheets, pillowcases, and so forth.

stucco Plaster or cement used for covering both interior and exterior walls. It usually leaves a rough, often extremely irregular surface. Stucco effects can be imitated by applying thick paint with a sponge.

stud Wood beam, perpendicular to the floor, to which the walls of interiors are nailed.

study Extra room, usually but not necessarily on the same floor as the living and dining room, designed for quiet work or reading. A study usually contains bookshelves and a desk. Also called *library* and *den*.

suite (sweet [correct pronunciation]; soot [industry pronunciation]) In furniture industry, pieces designed to go together, such as a dining table, buffet, and chairs all in the same style of furniture.

summer furniture Furniture suitable for use either inside or outside during the summer. Usually less formal than other furniture. Outdoor summer furniture should be impervious to weathering; see chapter 7, "Buying Today's New Furniture," for information on selecting such furniture. Indoor summer furniture — which is often used throughout the year on an enclosed porch, for instance — is often made of bamboo or rattan. White is a popular color for summer furniture frames, and upholstery fabrics often feature bold colors. Also called *casual furniture*, *leisure furniture*, *patio furniture*, and *outdoor furniture*.

swag Decorative draped fabric placed over a window and usually used with curtains or draperies. See also *jabot*.

swatch Small piece of fabric or wallpaper used as a sample. Swatches should be kept of all items being considered for use in the home to assure color coordination and to enable study of the colors under home lighting conditions.

switch plate Covering, usually metal or plastic, for wall light switches. Switch plates should be removed before painting or wallpapering. Many styles of decorative switch plates are available in home centers, hardware stores, and some department stores.

synthetic See *man-made*; *plastic*.

T

table lamp See under *lamp*.

table Flat-topped object supported by legs. Following is a list of common table types.

> **bedside table** Another name for nightstand. See *nightstand* under *end table*.
>
> **bridge table** See *card table*.
>
> **butler's tray table** Coffee table with four small drop leaf sides containing finger holes. The authentic butler's tray table is made in two sections so that the top part, the tray, can be lifted from the table. There are many adaptations of the table which do not have the tray feature. See also *coffee table*.
>
> **candlestand** Table, usually a little taller than chair arm height, with a small, usually round surface, originally designed to hold a candle. Today, these tables are also called *cigarette tables*.
>
> **card table** Small square table designed for playing games in which four people take part. Card tables are often made with folding legs so they can be easily stored when not needed. Also called *bridge table*.
>
> **chairside table** Another name for end table. See *end table*.
>
> **cigarette table** See *candlestand*.
>
> **cocktail table** See *coffee table*.
>
> **coffee table** Low, seat-height table placed in front of a sofa or chairs to hold magazines, ashtrays, coffee, and so forth. Many decorators feel that two small coffee tables with a walking space between are more useful than one large one in front of large sofas.
>
> **console** Originally, a legless table suspended from the wall. Now the term usually refers to a small waist-high table designed to be placed flat against the wall. Half-circle console tables are popular; two such tables may be combined to make a round dining table when needed. Some console tables have tilt-tops which open to enlarge the table. See *tilt-top table*.

dressing table Desklike table with large mirror for combing hair and applying makeup.

drop leaf table Table hinged on the sides so it can be made smaller by dropping one or two side sections down. When the table is open, leaves are supported by brackets or braces.

end table Flat-topped table which may contain drawers. These tables are the height of the arm of a sofa and placed at either end of a sofa or beside a chair. End tables are also used between twin beds and on either side of double beds as *bedside tables* or *nightstands*.

makeup table Another name for dressing table. See *dressing table*.

nest of tables Drawerless tables of descending size, the largest of which is usually the height of a chair arm; the two or more smaller tables fit snugly into the larger table.

Parsons table Table with legs at the outer corners, originally developed at the Parsons School of Design in New York City.

pedestal table Table with one central supporting leg (the pedestal) rather than three or more.

tilt-top table Usually round, designed with a top which can be moved from a horizontal to a vertical position. In the vertical position, a tilt-top table takes up less space and can be more easily stored. The tops are often decorated so they serve as a room accent when vertical.

tea cart See *serving cart*.

telephone bench Combination chair and table on which a telephone can be placed during conversation. There is usually also space for storing telephone books.

television Where you choose to place a television set is up to you. It should be placed so it can be seen from several sitting positions. General lighting should be left on while the set is in use. Television sets can be hidden when not in use behind cabinets; they can also be disguised by curtains. Television sets generate a great deal of heat, and sufficient ventilation must be provided to avoid the risk of fire. Portable television sets, while lighter than most other sets, are not as light as their name suggests.

tester See *canopy*.

tieback Anything used to hold a curtain or drapery to one side of a window. Tiebacks can be self-fabric, decorative trimming, fringe, or ornate metal. They are also called *holdbacks* and do not necessarily tie.

Tiffany lamp See under *lamp*.

tile Small squares or sections (measuring up to about twelve inches) which interlock or abut and are used to cover floors, walls, or ceilings. There is mirrored tile, ceramic tile, vinyl tile, even carpet tile. *Dutch tiles* are tiles from Holland or influenced by tiles from Holland and characterized by blue patterns. *Portuguese tiles* are usually larger than Dutch tiles and combine coloring such as bright blue and bright yellow. Most tiles have geometric designs and can be placed at any angle; there are also tiles which form a complete picture only when joined. See also chapter 12, "Room Back-grounds."

tilt-top table See under *table*.

toile *(twal)* Short for *toile de Jouy*, an upholstery and drapery fabric printed with one-color patterns of rustic scenes.

tufting See *tufted rug* under *rugs and carpets*.

U

under curtains See *glass curtains* under *curtains and draperies*.

unfinished furniture Furniture, almost always made of wood, which is sold unpainted and unfinished. At one time somewhat limited in styling, it is available today in many different styles. It can be found in department stores, shops specializing in it, and in catalogues from companies selling unfinished furniture in kit form by mail. Many firms offering unfinished furniture also offer a choice of finishes at an extra charge.

unpainted furniture See *unfinished furniture*.

upholstered furniture See chapter 8, "Buying Upholstered Furniture."

V

varnish See *paints, lacquers, and varnishes*.

veneer A thin layer of wood, usually chosen for its grain, laminated to other layers, usually of woods with less desirable grain. For a full discussion of veneer, see chapter 6, "Buying Wood Furniture."

Victorian Term used both of the reign of Queen Victoria of England (reigned 1835-1901) and of furniture and architecture developed during that time. Although many different styles came into being during the period the term most often refers to furniture made of dark woods (especially rosewood and mahogany), marble topped and highly decorated. See also chart, chapter 5, "What Is Period Furniture?"

vinyl See *plastic*.

vinyl wall coverings See *wall covering*; *wallpaper*.

W

walk-in closet See *closet*.

wall covering Anything used on the wall in the manner of wallpaper, covering a large expanse and serving a decorative purpose. Wall coverings may be fabric, prepasted vinyl with a paper backing (which peels off), or wallpaper. See also full discussion in chapter 12, "Room Backgrounds."

wall hanging Small area decoration which is hung on a wall; generally soft and flexible rather than rigid, as are pictures or mirrors. A hooked rug, made by a family member and hung on the wall instead of being placed on the floor, is a typical wall hanging.

wallpaper Paper, usually printed with a pattern, placed on the wall by means of some special adhesive. Prepasted wallpaper, with an adhesive activated by water, is available. Wallpaper often refers to wall coverings made of materials other than paper. For a full discussion, see chapter 12, "Room Backgrounds."

water bed See under *bed*.

welting Decorative edging which adds a degree of strength to the edge (usually a seam) where it is sewn. It is made by covering cord with strips of bias fabric.

whatnot See *bric-a-brac*.

whitewash Coating made of lime used to paint buildings white. True whitewash is rarely used today, but in provincial interiors the effect is imitated with certain paints.

white wood Another term for unfinished furniture. See *unfinished furniture*.

window Means by which light and air are admitted to a room.

window hangings Curtains and draperies. See *curtains and draperies*.

window treatment The way in which a window is decorated.

Windsor chair See under *chair*.

wood Product from trees used extensively for furniture. Wood is plentiful in most parts of the world and can be treated in various ways for different effects. For a full discussion, see chapter 6, "Buying Wood Furniture."

wrought iron See under *metal*.

Z

zipper Closure made of interlocking teeth or coils attached to fabric. Zippers are used for slipcovers and cushions so that the covers can be removed for cleaning and changing. See chapter 8, "Buying Upholstered Furniture" and chapter 11, "Fabrics for Home Furnishings."

Index

The index which follows is designed to help you in finding specific information in the chapters of this book. The dictionary section which is, of course, in alphabetical order, is not indexed.